Entrepreneur
VOICES
ON

STRATEGIC MANAGEMENT

The Staff of Entrepreneur Media, Inc.

Entrepreneur
PRESS

Entrepreneur Press, Publisher
Cover Design: Andrew Welyczko
Production and Composition: Eliot House Productions

This publication is designed to provide accurate and
authoritative information in regard to the subject matter covered.
It is sold with the understanding that the publisher is not
engaged in rendering legal, accounting or other professional
services. If legal advice or other expert assistance is required, the
services of a competent professional person should be sought.

Library of Congress Cataloging-in-Publication Data
    Names: Mintzer, Rich, author. | Entrepreneur Media, Inc.,
       author.
    Title: Entrepreneur voices on strategic management / by The
       Staff of Entrepreneur Media and Rich Mintzer.
    Description: Irvine, California: Entrepreneur Media, Inc.,
       [2018] | Series: Entrepreneur voices
    Identifiers: LCCN 2017043417| ISBN 978-1-59918-618-4 (alk.
       paper) | ISBN 1-59918-618-7 (alk. paper)
    Subjects: LCSH: Strategic planning.
    Classification: LCC HD30.28 .M5645 2018 | DDC 658.4/012—dc23
      LC record available at https://lccn.loc.gov/2017043417

Printed in the United States of America
22 21 20 19 18   10 9 8 7 6 5 4 3 2 1

CONTENTS

PART II
MANAGING PRODUCTIVITY

Contents

PART III
MANAGING EMPLOYEE PERFORMANCE

Contents

FOREWORD BY RIAZ KHADEM

Co-author of **Total Alignment: Tactics and Tools for Streamlining Your Organization**

The theme of the book is strategic management—a timely topic, as the world of management is changing and requires a new perspective. Gone are the days when a manager based his or her success solely on the ability to meet quotas or reach financial expectations. Now, management requires a more holistic approach to lead, to inspire, to empower, to provide conditions necessary for self-management, to avoid sacrificing the organization's long-term health in favor of short-term results, and yes—to get the most out of our employees. Specifically, we look to strategic management as the necessary orientation for all managers.

What, exactly is meant by "strategic?" In short, it's a management mindset in which you think critically, align with the vision and strategy of the organization, act purposefully, and plan accordingly. It means that you act strategically to fulfill not only the needs of those reporting to you, but also collaborate with your peers across silos that might exist.

Effective strategic managers work together with their teams and cross-functional relationships on a constant basis to respond to questions that all companies have:

- Who are we? What are our core values?

- What's our purpose? What do we do and why? What is our mission?

- What does our future look like? What is our vision of the future?

- How do we get to that future? What is our strategy?

- How do we execute? How can we implement our strategy?

Foreword by Riaz Khadem

- How do we stay the course? How do we maintain alignment?

For me, the concepts, tactics, and tools for responding to these questions emerged from many years working in the management trenches with companies all over the world. I have seen managers who were confused about directions they were receiving from above and the needs they saw on the ground. I have worked with managers who were stressed from being micromanaged, and who were executing plans they had devised and then were forced to change them. I have observed managers who acted like robots, simply passing on directives from upper management to their direct reports without assisting them to understand and own those directives.

The confusion, stress, and the indifference I saw in those managers prompted me to develop the system (and book) known as *Total Alignment*, where managers can be both strategic and aligned, where the organization works toward a unified purpose, a clear vision, and a strategy aligned with the vision. Individuals are accountable for their contribution to vision and strategy. They have clearly defined responsibilities supported by key information to track their progress. Individual competencies are aligned with their accountabilities. Behaviors are

Foreword by Riaz Khadem

congruent with values. Teams at the right levels are empowered to develop and implement action plans to improve results. Cross-functional responsibilities are clearly defined, and spaces are provided for joint resolution of problems, so silos disappear.

The book you are reading on Strategic Management contains a wealth of ideas from distinguished authors on the subject of management, including voices of those who address many of the same issues I see in my work every day. You will find useful information on a variety of topics including: promotion of accountability, managing productivity, decentralizing management, boosting retention, avoiding the fear of making mistakes, workplace diversity, and tips for giving feedback, among others.

You're reading this book because you want to learn how to be a better manager, a strategic partner, and a great asset to the organization you are working for. You know that effective management is crucial to workforce productivity and employee retention, not to mention its impact on your corporate culture.

I encourage you to study and reflect on the many useful concepts presented in this book with special attention to concepts for delegating the right tasks to the right people, avoiding micromanagement, giving useful feedback, and motivating your team so your company can thrive in today's challenging market. The fine editors and writers at Entrepreneur are sharing useful concepts about management. They bring you great advice, reflections, and tips that will help you become the manager your company and your team deserve.

MANAGERS: MAINTAINING A DELICATE BALANCE

Modern-day managers are not in an easy position and hence often do not receive the credit they deserve. Managers walk the tightrope between founders, owners, and other higher-ups on one side and employees on the other—not to mention customers who typically turn to a manager when there is a discrepancy but rarely say, "job well done."

Despite maintaining this delicate balance, a good manager can stand out on both sides of the equation. In fact, leadership depends on good managers: the two go hand in hand. Employees benefit from good managers who go beyond assigning tasks and provide a reason and a purpose behind their requests. The best managers see the vision of the owner(s) and bring it to life by training, developing, nurturing, supporting, providing feedback, and encouraging employees. The owners and the CEO have long-term plans, but the manager must make those plans a reality with the help of a strong, enthusiastic team.

For years, managers were supposed to focus more attention on the structure, systems, procedures, and tasks at hand. Business leaders would set the course, and the managers had to guide the vessel forward at all costs. That is no longer how managers define their jobs. In the current state of business (at least in most businesses), effective managers play an integral role in leading their employees by actually connecting with them—not just the roles that need to be filled or the tasks that need to be completed. As a result of this more humanized approach, employees respond to more relatable managers and perform at a much higher level.

Managers still need to keep a close eye on the ROI and a wide variety of metrics for monitoring the financial well-being of the company. But the position has expanded significantly into a leadership role in which a manager can excel by effectively understanding, communicating (which includes listening), motivating, and evaluating everyone working for them. This includes providing a range of feedback, from constructive criticism to praise. It also covers knowing how to get the best out of people by recognizing their similarities, differences, and unique capabilities in addition to their shortcomings. Managers who understand which people excel, or fall short, in specific areas can use that knowledge wisely and get the best out of each person, not unlike a baseball manager who knows who should play shortstop, centerfield, and catcher.

In the upcoming articles, there is a strong emphasis on the human side of management. After all, technology notwithstanding, people remain at the core of all business. From understanding the impact of the right culture, to knowing how to give feedback, to transparency, diversity, and accountability, managers need to know a lot to succeed today. Good managers try to learn and juggle all these areas. Great managers have already mastered and embraced them.

MANAGING YOUR EGO

The modern-day manager needs to know how to manage those who are close in physical proximity and those working from remote locations. The trick is to find a balance between using a telescope and a microscope. The manager who is too far away from what is taking place in the office is usually unable to communicate effectively or too late on timing when it comes to vital day-to-day decisions.

Conversely, being too close is not the way to encourage trust or autonomy or build confidence. "Micromanagement is the destroyer of momentum," writes Miles Anthony Smith in his book *Why Leadership Sucks Volume 2*, and he is right. The result of living in a free country is that people, by and large, do not like being controlled, and "micromanagement" is business-speak for too much control. Employees need to recognize the need for authority and acknowledge guidelines and rules because disorder and chaos are unwanted. But when it comes down to "control," most of us draw a mental red line.

Of course, managers who are controlling are not always aware of their actions. Micromanagement is often ego-driven, but for that matter, so is delegation. Micromanagement usually means you think nobody can do it as well as you, and the inability to delegate means the same thing. Managers must, therefore, "get over it" when it comes to their own ego-centricity. Of course, this is easier said than done. While many individuals can take a closer look at themselves in the mirror and do a self-assessment to find their shortcomings or weaknesses, truly ego-centric managers may see someone doing a great job, even if that is not the truth. We can all think of individuals who stood in their own way of success, because everything was all about them. Even if things are going poorly, they don't see it. The bottom line is that at some point, the manager will need to be told they have to shift gears and focus their attention on the team.

A manager needs to explain tasks, especially when technology is involved, and they need to explain the desired outcome. They need to communicate what is needed and when, and for greater clarity, why the task is necessary in the bigger picture. A manager needs to know when to exercise self-control and not be impulsive, as well as when to step away and let the employee(s) do their jobs. If they were hired for their expertise in the field or trained sufficiently in-house, they should be able to run with the ball.

Resisting the tendency to micromanage, as well as knowing when to delegate, comes from a degree of trust. Do you trust that, left on their own, the individual(s) you supervise can complete the task or not? If you, as the manager, need to be involved every step of the way, you are never going to find out if they can or cannot handle the job. At some point in the process, you will need to let go, just as parents need to take their hands off the bicycle and let their children ride without training wheels. It's worth noting that trust issues usually stem more from the manager than the employee. Unless someone has given you clear-cut reasons to mistrust them, you need to be able to let go of that bicycle and let your employee ride. If they fall, guess what? They'll get up and try again.

When it comes to delegating, you also need to harness your ego, or at least tell yourself, "If the team succeeds, I can enjoy their success." Remember, delegating is also all about trust. Can someone do the job as well, or almost as well, as you can and get the same results? If so, then delegate the responsibilities to that person and free yourself to do bigger and better things for the business (OK so that's a little ego-stroking, but it's also true).

1

SEVEN WARNING SIGNS YOU'RE THE DREADED MICROMANAGER

Aaron Haynes

Micromanagers are notorious for causing high-stress levels, low morale, loss of productivity, and dread in the office, among other negative repercussions. In fact, they are every employee's worst nightmare. A micromanaging boss kills efficiency with outdated, self-centered, and under-developed management methods.

But to be fair, no manager is queuing up for this undesirable role. In fact, most fear turning into a micromanager. The line between an efficient manager and a micromanager is sometimes blurred, and it's easy to cross it, unaware you're on a slippery slope to becoming a dysfunctional boss.

Let's look at the signal characteristics of a micromanager in the making:

1. *You're scared of losing control.* Because of your need to control, you're obsessed with knowing what staffers are doing, and everything must be done your way or you're not satisfied. Therefore, you often call back work you assign because it's not up to your standards. On top of that, you dish out instructions but make it impossible for your team to input their own ideas. As a result, you stifle their creativity, communication, and self-development, while leaving no option for effective productivity. Holding on tightly to control out of fear will eventually cause you to lose it in the end.

2. *You alone have the best approach to every task.* Believing you know best, you view your employees' work as inferior. Therefore, your actions scream that their work is substandard, a strong sign that you're micromanaging. You don't give them the opportunity to use

their skills, talents, and know-how. Instead, you implement all the ideas, take control of communicating with clients, and make decisions based on your knowledge. Believing you have all the answers for resolving tasks, you work on them solo. This attitude pushes employees aside, causing them to doubt their own capabilities.

3. *You're itching to lead.* Leading is not a bad thing. On the other hand, a forceful boss who is unwilling to negotiate, who is always interfering, and who is unable to offer flexibility is a poor leader. Continual interference is a sign you lack confidence in your employees. Nevertheless, there are times when it's necessary to lead, especially in large financial transactions, vital decision-making, or other important business areas requiring managerial authority. However, if you're always in the driver's seat and find it difficult to allow employees to manage everyday tasks, this creates uncertainty and resentment. As an alternative, train staff, build trust, and support them.

4. *You suspect everybody wastes time and resources.* One of the most annoying traits of a micro-manager is their suspicion. Because you

suspect everyone is either wasting time or company resources, you are always prying. You command a detailed record of phone calls, meetings, spending, tasks, or anything else you think could be wasted. This obsession brings stress on everyone. Constantly judging and prying will eventually create lack of faith in you and drive employees out of the company.

5. *You organize endless, unnecessary meetings.* Micromanagers use any excuse to call for a meeting. Usually, these meetings are nothing to do with work productivity. They are a pretext for finding irrelevant faults. Or you attend meetings to get your points across in discussions that don't require your presence. Another sign is insisting all employees attend meetings, whether the topic is relevant to them or not. Unnecessary, drawn-out meetings end up wasting precious time, cutting into efficiency, and breeding confusion.

6. *You second-guess the practice of delegating.* Everyone has the same amount of time during the day. However, your time seems less than others. Could this be because you don't know how to delegate? Each day, you're

overloaded with trivial tasks and projects that rarely get completed. Lack of delegation and communication with your employees forces you to micromanage rather than distribute responsibilities. Instead of retracting delegated tasks, allow employees to handle jobs within their capability. Practice developing your delegation skills to reduce your workload and give employees a sense of ownership.

7. *You're trying to run a one-person show.* Perhaps you have the attitude that micromanagement means taking on everything by yourself. Consequently, you lack faith in your employees' abilities and bear the brunt of the workload. You're busy fretting about their productivity and criticizing their work, leaving you little time to manage properly. Rather than working with them to develop a competent team, you set them up to depend on you. This leads to increased workload and bigger pressures on you, amplifying the danger of impending burnout.

Finally, perhaps you have good intentions at heart but still cross the line over into becoming a micromanager. If you identified with any of the earlier danger signs, you are now in a better position to improve your management skills. One way to improve working relationships is to get regular feedback from staff. Reflect on the response, measure yourself against their comments, and take action to implement the necessary changes. Transform yourself from being a dreaded micromanager to becoming a valued, respected leader.

2

EITHER YOU RUN THE ORGANIZATION OR THE ORGANIZATION WILL RUN YOU

Jim Joseph

A boss several years ago gave me a very important piece of advice without even realizing it. I was asking him what hadn't worked out with my predecessor, and he responded with a one-sentence answer that has stuck with me ever since:

"He didn't run the organization; the organization ran him."

At the time, it struck me as such a simple concept, so why would anyone not get it? How could you possibly "let the organization run you?"

Boy, was I in for a surprise. The organization was in chaos at the time. There were no priorities, only deadlines. There were no plans, only panic attacks. There was no order.

That's no way to run an organization, yet everyone was running ragged.

My boss did me a huge favor in that one statement . . . he summed up what I needed to do in my first 30, 60, and 90 days.

I needed to prioritize the group's work, I needed to put plans in place, and I needed to establish some order to the work flows and demands of the organization. Because my boss made that one statement to me, I didn't get caught up in the demands, deliverables, and drills that could have easily gotten me off to a bad start, just like my predecessor. If I hadn't paid attention to that piece of advice, I might have also gotten caught up in a runaway train and perhaps never gotten control of it.

It's so important to not let the demands of the day run you around, constantly forcing your priorities and putting your plans on the back burner. If you let the fire drills take control, you'll never get far enough ahead of the workload to be able to run the organization.

The organization will run you.

So, how do you avoid this common mistake?

Delegate to Others

As a business leader, it's important to not get too caught up in the work. That's what the teams are for. Let your teams manage the details and the deadlines so that you can focus more on the big picture. You can be a consultant to the team, for sure, but you don't have to do their work for them. By delegating, you can allow yourself time and space to step back and take a broader look at the organization. Now, you can work *on* the business rather than spending so much time working *in* the business. To use another sports analogy, you can be more effective as a manager if you are on the sidelines rather than in the middle of the action. That's why delegating work to others is so important.

Determine Firm Milestones

For key initiatives you are driving, it's important to determine firm milestones and stick to them. Don't let the demands of the day push back your timelines. Give project coordinators firm deadlines to meet, and treat them like you'd treat any other business priority. If you let yourself get into "crisis mode" whenever some new business interrupts the flow of business, you will find that the organization starts moving ahead of you. It's important to remain in control, allow teams to help put out fires, and stick to the milestones you have set up.

Dedicate Time

Let's face it, the days and the weeks and the months can get away from us. Sometimes, there's no avoiding the pressures of the moment. That's why it's so important to set aside time each day to do your own work . . . the work you need to do to run the organization. For me, it's the early morning hours that work best to do my own work. But everyone is different, and everyone needs to find their own way. Often, managers neglect their own work while trying to manage others, and as a result, it becomes like chasing a train down the track—work doesn't stop and you can't get caught up. You need to carve out your own time. None of this is easy. As my dad says, "They wouldn't call it work if it was easy." But it's a lot harder if you have an organization that is running you rather than the other way around. Heed the strong advice given to me back in the day, and you'll see your work produce better results.

FIVE KEYS TO PROMOTING ACCOUNTABILITY IN YOUR BUSINESS

Martin Zwilling

It's easy to emphasize accountability with your team, but not so easy to tell them *how* to be accountable. It's even harder to make them *want* to be accountable—especially since many business leaders forget they are the role models for accountability. And, in fact, they don't audit their own actions to make sure they always practice what they preach.

It's also imperative that accountability become more than a buzzword, which is continuously bantered about. It needs to be a cornerstone of the employer-employee relationship. Like most aspects of business, accountability must start at the top with leaders and managers saying what they will do and doing what they have said.

I recently read Subir Chowdhury's *The Difference: When Good Enough Isn't Enough*, which shines a light on both of these issues. Chowdhury is one of the world's leading management consultants, and he argues that accountability is only one part of a caring culture that must be built and maintained to achieve sustainable, competitive improvement.

The other key parts of a caring culture include nurturing employees and leaders who are straightforward, thoughtful, and resolute in their approach to the business. All my years of experience in business resonate with that assessment and allow entrepreneurs to explain to team members what accountability means and what steps are required to get there:

1. *Be willing to proclaim that something needs to be done*. We all know of examples where employees and managers see the same problem occur over and over again but never raise a flag about it. Being accountable for doing something, or for changing something, needs to start by addressing what needs to be done

or changed and making a conscientious effort to take the lead on an action step.

2. *Accept personal responsibility for tackling an issue.* Apathetic people are quick to point the finger at someone else or defer by saying "It's not my job." Leaders must send the message—and show by example—that finding quality solutions to meet the needs of customers is everyone's job no matter how large the business. People must understand that customers are at the root of the company's success, and those working on problems must be rewarded.

3. *Make positive choices or decisions to act.* Employees who don't think they have enough training or sense of the mission will shy away from making big decisions, which is vital for accountability. Make sure your company empowers its employees through positivity and a sense of trust.

4. *Think deeply about the consequences of each choice.* Are you working to get a problem off your back, or are you only serving your ego? Are you creating the best long-term solution for the customer, or are you merely using an expedient solution? Think before you act.

5. *Set high expectations for yourself and your team.* When you set your own sights high, you cannot help but inspire others. When you know others are taking their lead from you, it's easier to stay accountable. Inspired team members will then set their own targets higher, and that momentum will lead to better customer experiences and business success.

To make a real difference in your business, you need to be the role model for accountability. This begins by nurturing a caring mindset across the entire organization. Here are three things you need to look for in order to develop and exhibit such a caring mindset:

1. *Direct and open communication.* Managers need to be transparent with their team and encourage the team to be straightforward with them and with each other. Communication suffers when people don't trust that they will be treated fairly. Too often, leaders hide business realities and personal mistakes, but expect everyone else to understand and do the right thing. Remember, everything starts at the top, including openness, communication, and trust.

2. *Individual empathy and thoughtful listening.* Real listening involves not just hearing what others say, but trying to put yourself in their shoes and fully understand the message. For managers, this requires getting out from behind their desks, visiting factory floors, meeting with employees, and being accessible at any time to their team.

3. *Passion and perseverance.* Every problem can be resolved with a mindset of passion, determination, and perseverance, and every situation can be improved. It requires humility and a willingness to change and adapt—even an acceptance that continuous improvement is the norm—but it's worth it. Passionate people don't ever settle for less than their personal best.

Accountability isn't easy. It can't be accomplished by edict, but it can be taught through example by leaders who practice the principles they want their team to follow—leaders who build a mindset of caring throughout the organization. How long has it been since you took a look in the mirror at yourself and asked if you've held yourself accountable and done what you set out (and told others) that you would do?

ENTREPRENEUR VOICES SPOTLIGHT: INTERVIEW WITH KARIM ABOUELNAGA

After securing more than $300,000 in college scholarships, Karim Abouelnaga attended Cornell University's School of Hotel Administration, where he received his bachelor's degree. He is currently pursuing his master's degree in Education Policy Analysis from Teacher's College at Columbia University.

It was, however, at the age of 18, while at Cornell, that Karim founded Practice Makes Perfect with five fellow Cornell students. A nonprofit, Practice Makes Perfect narrows the achievement gap by providing low-income students with mentorship and resources that are beyond the reach of their inner-city public schools. Starting throughout the five boroughs of New York City in 2010, Practice Makes Perfect has worked to bridge the "learning lag" during summer vacations by providing summer education programs that have benefitted more than 550 youngsters, while helping many more through outreach programs.

Entrepreneur: How did you develop the right mix of controls and autonomy to create the best culture for Practice Makes Perfect?

Abouelnaga: Trial and error. I did a lot of reading on best practices from some of the most successful entrepreneurs and executives over the past century. Then, I started to try and test them out to see which ones I liked and which ones made the most sense for how I wanted to operate our company.

Entrepreneur: When it comes to balancing their own work and responsibilities of the team(s), how do you recommend managers take control of these dual roles in their business before the business takes control of them?

Abouelnaga: Being in middle management is one of the toughest things in the world. You're dealing with pressure from the top as things are constantly changing, yet you're trying to convey stability to everyone at the bottom, and you're dealing with your own work. I recommend that managers "manage up." Keep the lines of communication open with your superiors. They have resources and relationships that can help remove obstacles from your path or find ways to make your life easier. Most managers do it all the time for their direct reports, but they forget to look for that from the leaders they report to. If you don't make it a priority, you risk being compressed in the middle from all of the pressure coming from the top and the bottom.

Entrepreneur: How and when should managers determine it's time to delegate jobs or responsibilities, and then how do they hold people accountable without micro-managing?

Abouelnaga: Generally, once a job or a responsibility conflicts with a bigger goal, or they have a pretty good handle on it and can easily explain it to someone else, it's time to delegate. Accountability is set through culture. There needs to be positive reinforcement present that managers can use when things go according to plan. The absence of it is punishment enough when people do not deliver. With that in mind, I always advise that managers set check-in points on projects, with more frequent check-ins at the beginning to ensure their direct reports are moving in the right direction. Then, they should have more frequent check-ins again toward the end as the finishing touches are being put on. If managers know when the deadlines are, then they shouldn't be checking in before that, unless their direct reports ask them to.

Entrepreneur: Can managers hold too many meetings, or check-ins, and if so, when should they pull back?

Abouelnaga: Yes, there is such a thing as too many meetings. Generally, I think one 20- to 30-minute one-on-one check-in per week, to see how people are doing personally and professionally, plus one larger hour-and-half meeting with a team to discuss challenges and strategies, also weekly, are more than enough. Managers should ask direct reports for a weekly email that includes challenges/concerns and successes/opportunities. We've been doing them at Practice Makes Perfect for years now. It really allows us to focus on what matters.

Entrepreneur: Why the name Practice Makes Perfect, and what overall message do you want to convey to youngsters in your programs?

Abouelnaga: Ultimately, we wanted to convey to youngsters that the time and the effort that you put into something is what dictates the outcome. The more time and effort you put into something, the better you're going to do at it.

4

MICROMANAGEMENT IS MURDER—STOP KILLING YOUR EMPLOYEES

Heather R. Huhman

I need to get something off my chest. Early in my career, when I first had employees working for me, I was a micromanager. It's not something I'm proud of, but I was so focused on how their work reflected on me as a manager that I found it difficult to overcome my need to control what they did.

And that wasn't wise. Instead of nurturing my employees' strengths, my micromanagement was driving a wedge between me and them. Every day, I could see the unnecessary stress I was putting on everyone. Had I continued down that path, the consequences might have been deadly. Literally.

While the negative health impacts of high-stress jobs have been known for years, new research has found that mixing that stress with micromanagement increases the odds of employees' early deaths.

A 2017 study from the Indiana University Kelley School of Business looked at how stress and levels of control affected 2,363 employees. When comparing highly demanding jobs, those that also gave employees less control were associated with a 15.4 percent increased chance of death.

While no one wishes an early grave on their employees, micromanagers can still find it difficult to loosen the reins. Instead of thinking about the control being given up, however, they should focus on what will be gained by "backing off."

Here are five ways to trade in micromanagement for a healthier and more productive leadership style:

1. Include Employees in the Goal-Setting

At the heart of my own micromanagement tendencies was the fear that my employees would make me look bad. If they failed, that outcome would tell our boss that I was a failure. Because of that fear, the goals I set for my staffers weren't based on their individual potential, but rather what I wanted from them. Understandably, they weren't exactly motivated.

The key, then, is to get employees involved with a goal-setting process so they can see purpose in their work. Unfortunately, that sense of accomplishment is something many lack.

The 2016 *Employee Job Satisfaction and Engagement* report from the Society for Human Resource Management (SHRM) looked at how 600 employees felt about their jobs. Only 30 percent of respondents were satisfied with how their work contributed to the overall success of the company.

The message? Sit down and have a conversation with employees about the organization's goals. Instead of telling them what numbers they need to hit, ask them how they can help contribute to the bigger picture. That will give the team more independence and ownership over the value of their accomplishments.

2. Foster a Two-Way Conversation

One of the biggest issues with micromanagement is that it's one-sided. Everything has to be done the manager's way, which is probably why the aforementioned SHRM survey found that only 37 percent of employees participating said they were very satisfied with the respect and consideration their managers gave their ideas.

Remember, there's more than one way to skin a cat, and employees might even know the best way.

Instead of barking orders, ask employees for their ideas and opinions. Discuss how they work best and how they can work most efficiently. If they see a different way to do things, let them give it a shot. After all, as long as they get the job done and do it well, what does it matter if they choose a different method?

3. Cut Ties with the Office

Flexible and remote work options are scary for micromanagers. It takes employees out of their line of sight and away from their control. But the truth is that most employees are more productive when they're given the freedom to work where they'd like.

In a 2016 FlexJobs survey of more than 3,100 professionals, 65 percent said they worked better in a location outside of the traditional office. Whether that's because employees want to get away from office distractions or because they feel more inspired working in a coffee shop, micromanagers need to unchain employees from their desks.

Accept that employees might work better when no one is looking over their shoulder, and let them work where they want. This will give them more professional independence and take away your own temptation to micromanage.

4. Make Employee Recognition Personal

There's an inherent disconnect in most employee-recognition programs. Sure, employees are acknowledged, but even their rewards are micromanaged. Rewards are chosen by management or other company leaders, making these honors less than meaningful to employees.

However, when employees get to choose their own recognition, it's more effective. That's what makes recognition platforms like Blueboard stand out.

Blueboard allows managers to reward employees, but employees choose how to redeem those rewards. They can choose from a variety of experiences that enrich their lives—spa treatments, tickets to a sporting event, or countless other memorable events that actually mean something to them.

Instead of acknowledging employees in a way that management dictates should make them feel good, they can choose their own satisfaction. That makes the recognition more personal and more motivating.

5. Focus Feedback on Results

Great feedback allows employees to learn and grow. If a manager simply says, "You need to do things this way instead," employees feel controlled. They're not being guided; they're being micromanaged.

A better option is to focus on facts and results rather than the process. For instance, if a goal of winning ten new accounts has been set, have feedback revolve around whether or not those expectations have been met. Employees can look at their results and think about whether or not their process worked as well as they'd hoped. They can see what they're doing right and what's leading to their success, as well as how they need to adapt.

This type of feedback gives them more control over how they improve. It's more collaborative than being told what they're doing "right" or "wrong."

Micromanagement can be tempting, especially for new leaders. The less control employees have, the lower the chances for unwanted surprises. But in reality, micromanaging is bad for employees and bad for company productivity. Remember that before getting overly involved with how employees do their work.

INCREASE ACCOUNTABILITY WITHOUT BREATHING DOWN PEOPLE'S NECKS

Karim Abouelnaga

One of the toughest balances to achieve within an organization is between building a culture that gives people space while maintaining an environment of accountability. The line between managing and micromanaging is very fine and in some cases blurry. At Practice Makes Perfect, we've operated with an unlimited vacation policy for almost a year now. We close our offices for every federal holiday and have a compulsory two days off that everyone has to take per quarter to recharge. In order to operate with this level of flexibility, we have to ensure that controls are in place so that work gets done. More important, we don't want to stifle creativity.

Here is how we ensure accountability without breathing down everyone's neck:

Create Annual Goals

Every year, we set three to five goals that everyone in the entire company rallies behind. At the end of the year, those are the only goals that matter. We know we are done with our planning when we can respond "yes" to the following question: if we looked back at the end of the year and this is all that we accomplished, would we be satisfied? A resounding, "yes," is required before we settle. It is also important to limit yourself to five. If you have too many priorities, then nothing becomes a priority.

Develop Quarterly Objectives

Every department leader sets objectives that stem from the annual goals we set for the company. Each department will also set departmentwide objectives. The objectives are then assigned to managers within the department who are responsible for delegating and project managing throughout the course of the quarter. The managers are accountable for the objectives, and their teams are responsible for delivering on them.

As a company, we also have a quarterly critical number (one key priority that can be measured and tracked that will move the company forward). The critical number is the most important priority for everyone within the company. We tie incentives during our quarterly celebration to our level of success at achieving our critical number. At the end of the quarter, we reflect on the critical number from the previous quarter and then share the critical number for the following quarter.

In an effort to document our journey and increase transparency, I also write a quarterly letter where I reflect on the things that went well and the things that didn't go as planned throughout the quarter. It also allows me to solicit help and anticipate what we have ahead of us for the following quarter.

Focus on Monthly Targets

Every month, we update a Key Performance Indicator (KPI) dashboard that is managed by the executive team. Once it is populated, we reflect on it with the company leadership team, and then, I put together an email to the entire company that includes the dashboard and comments on how we are doing toward our annual goals. This creates an incredible amount of accountability and transparency within the organization. Everyone has access to this document, and they easily see how we are managing our expenses, how much revenue we're bringing in, and what our company's burn rate is in that given moment. The executive team then holds a monthly town hall for people to bring up any questions or concerns they may have.

Have Weekly Emails

Toward the end of every week, we ask everyone in the organization to send a brief email to their manager. The email has three sections: challenges, successes, and a third section for anything the manager or company should start/stop/continue. If the person manages a budget, they also update any revenue or expense numbers. This should take no longer than 15 minutes. They are meant to be short and sweet, with the purpose of really shedding light on key items.

Once a week, every manager will also have a 10- to 20-minute check-in with their direct reports. Though they are fairly unstructured, they are opportunities to talk through the challenges in a weekly report, check in on any needs a team member may have in order to carry out their job, and discuss professional development opportunities. When we check in, I like to speak with my direct reports about the items I keep on a running list occurring throughout the week.

Do Daily Check-Ins

Every morning at 9:05 A.M., we have a group huddle. Everyone present in the office (we're 15 people now; if we were 20, we'd split in half) forms a circle, and they come prepared to share the most significant thing that happened the day before, the most important thing (just one) that they will accomplish that day, and whether or not they foresee anything slowing them down. This usually takes us between seven and ten minutes. It also provides us an opportunity to share any important companywide announcements as they come up instead of trying to create a meeting with a long agenda or sending a handful of emails. For people who have a 9 A.M. meeting or are working from home, we have an organization huddle channel on Slack. The daily huddles allow us to collaborate and troubleshoot potential bottlenecks before they arise.

From annual goals to daily check-ins, you want to maintain a strong sense of purpose and of communication so that nobody feels unsure of their role in the organization. This is how we hold people accountable. Of course, the schedule will differ based on the logistics of each business, especially with people working from remote locations. The key is to have ongoing accountability without, as noted earlier, breathing down people's necks.

6

SHOULD YOU DELEGATE THAT? A COMPREHENSIVE GUIDE

Larry Alton

Delegating tasks is an important, yet tricky, art in the realm of entrepreneurship. It's a way to lighten your workload and distribute tasks among your employees and partners, and if you do it right, you'll end up more productive as an organization. Plus, you'll be less stressed on a personal level.

Unfortunately, though, most entrepreneurs struggle to get delegating right. They don't know when to do it or how to do it, and they end up either never delegating at all or delegating so ineffectively that they wind up with more on their plates than when they started.

So, what should you do when you're faced with the ultimate dilemma: "Should I delegate that?" Here are the steps to take to answer that question.

Recognize Your Own Biases

Your first job is to recognize any internal biases that may be affecting your decision to delegate:

- *Control*. Many entrepreneurs see their business as "their baby," and want to do everything they can for the business. Unfortunately, this makes many entrepreneurs reluctant—or even stubborn—when it comes to delegating their responsibilities. If this is you, you need to learn how to let go of control.

- *Frugality*. It's tempting, especially when yours is a bootstrapped startup, to try to minimize costs as much as possible. Accordingly, you may avoid new hires or freelancers; however, as you'll see, this too has a cost associated with it.

- *Bothers*. Maybe you're trying to be a kind boss and don't want to increase the workloads of others. But, remember: it's your job to assign priorities, and depending on the structure of your business, your subordinates can likely delegate further.

Determine the Value of Your Time

The key first step in deciding whether to delegate something is determining the value of your time. How much do you make per hour as a consulting rate? If you don't charge a consulting rate, how much do you imagine yourself making at a similar position somewhere else?

Once you have a rough idea of how much your time is worth at an hourly rate, you'll know the relative "value of your time," which you can use to make more effective delegating decisions.

Categorize Needed Tasks as Short-Term and Long-Term Responsibilities

Next, you'll need to determine whether the challenge you're facing consists of short-term or long-term responsibilities. For example, if your business needs a new internet provider, you probably won't want to make another switch for a long time. That makes this a short-term responsibility, so whoever you delegate this task to will only have to research companies like Verizon and AT&T once.

However, if you're trying to manage a repair at a secondary property, know that you'll likely face a similar issue in the near future, so settle on a longer-term solution, such as a new hire or a property-management service to take over. If the cost to delegate to an outside source is still less than your hourly rate, hire that source.

Determine Your Priorities

Of course, you'll also have to determine your priorities as an entrepreneur. What do you currently have on your plate? Is there a major project that only you can work on at the top of the list? If so, consider any other tasks on your agenda as secondary and worthy of being delegated. However, if all your priorities are balanced, you may not need to consider delegating at all.

Review Your Staff Availability

You'll need to think about who's available to take over your work as well. Who on your team has the bandwidth to take over some of your work, and who is also making a lower relative hourly rate than you? If nobody on your team currently meets those criteria, think about hiring a freelancer from a service like Upwork or attempt to find a new hire on a site like Monster to fill the void.

Create a Quick Checklist

If these considerations are too abstract for you, here's a quick checklist to run down if you're considering delegating a task:

- *Is your task list too long?* Do you have too much to do? Check your biases and stresses here, and if the answer is yes, continue.

- *Can this be delegated right now?* If you can delegate a particular task to someone who knows how to do it, excellent. That's one less thing to worry about.

- *Can this be delegated cost effectively?* If you delegate the task to an employee, freelancer, or management service, will it cost less than it would if you were the one taking care of it? Will you pay less than your relative hourly rate? If so, delegating it is worthwhile.

- *Will this be a problem again; and if so, is it a problem worth preventing?* If nobody knows how to do the necessary tasks, and your training or hiring will cost more than your hourly rate, consider the future value that training will have.

Chances are, if you're thinking about delegating a task, it's worth finding a way to do so. You're busy and your time is valuable, so any time you can delegate work for less total cost than you'd spend doing it yourself, pull the trigger.

Finally, remember this: much of your job as a leader isn't task-by-task execution; it's setting a course for others to do what they do best.

MANAGING YOUR EGO—REFLECTIONS

When it comes down to it, micromanaging creates more stress and lowers productivity. As mentioned in Chapter 4, some 65 percent of those surveyed said they worked better in a location outside of the traditional office.

As a manager, you need to look for signs that you are micromanaging and put a greater emphasis on results rather than being involved in each step of the process. You need to let people show you what they are capable of doing and then provide guidance if necessary and personalized employee recognition when the goals or milestones are reached.

Not only do you want to step back when it comes to micromanaging, but you want to recognize the importance of delegating. By handing off specific jobs and responsibilities to others, you can let your team manage the details while you serve as a consultant. By stepping back, you also increase productivity. And by lightening your own load, you will be able to focus on the big picture while reducing your own level of stress. Additionally, you will be able to stay one step ahead of your business, focusing on what needs to be done to move the business forward rather than having the business get ahead of you. After all, you want to be running the business rather than the other way around.

Accountability also factors into the equation. By giving people more space to do their work autonomously, you create a more engaged culture. Employees feel a sense of greater responsibility. However, you do need to stay on top of what is and is not getting accomplished. Are goals being met? Milestones reached?

Setting annual goals and developing quarterly objectives and monthly targets are among the suggested means of keeping everyone moving in the same direction at a similar pace. You then need to check in on how everyone is doing. While daily check-ins first thing every morning may go over as well as micromanaging, it is easy to have ongoing communication through emails, meetings, one-on-ones, and regular reporting. Transparency and open communication are most important when it comes to accountability. Everyone needs to be on the same page to move forward as an organization. Of course, all of the above hinges on not being guided by your own ego and instead being humble, being accessible, and having a high level of trust. If managers trust their teams, with everyone (managers included) being held accountable for reaching their goals and the lines of communication open, the business is far more likely to see increased productivity. And in the end, this is a boost for everyone's ego.

MANAGING PRODUCTIVITY

There are several tips to making life as a manager easier. The simplest is to care about your employees. If you are able to find ways to make their lives better, you will make your job easier and end up with better results to boot.

By effectively managing productivity, you will see greater results, and employees will see the fruits of their labor. This is because increased productivity starts a chain reaction, whereby employees work harder, the business sees increased sales, and the profits benefit both the company and the employees—through higher salaries and more perks. But it starts with the production manager using systems and processes that can be easily mastered.

Managers need to find a fine line between "all business all the time" and coddling employees. You are there to perform a job and get increased productivity, but you are also there to manage other people. As such, your success is predicated on others. Therefore, like a good teacher, you want "A" students or employees rather than "D" students or employees who might make your job tougher.

Today, you will also, most likely, have to manage remote workers. In this case, communication is especially important. The tools of technology make it easier than ever to work with offsite employees. However, phone calls and face-to-face meetings should be part of the game plan. Managers have to remember that just because someone is not physically present does not mean they do not need feedback, answers to tough questions, and an occasional pat on the back. Workers can be highly productive from anyplace as long as they feel a part of the company and see the benefits of their productivity.

Within the physical office environment, there are also various factors that can affect a team's success and productivity. This includes the office layout, the office hierarchy—or lack thereof—rules and regulations, the office culture, and the opportunity for some much-needed downtime.

Clearly, there is a lot more to managing than timesheets and the numbers produced in a given week, month, quarter, or year. In the following chapters, six writers expound on ways to improve workplace efficiency, which goes hand in hand with increased productivity.

FIVE REASONS WHY WORKPLACE ANXIETY IS COSTING YOUR BUSINESS A FORTUNE

Quentin Vennie

A 2005 study conducted by the National Institute of Mental Health reports that over 40 million Americans are dealing with some form of an anxiety disorder. With over 18 percent of the U.S. population having been diagnosed with anxiety, a large majority have cited their workplace as a major contributor.

Anxiety is the most common form of mental illness in the country. Most people can identify with being stressed or having felt anxious at some point based on certain life events, such as starting a new job, moving to a new state, or giving a big presentation. However, it's important to note the differentiating factors between healthy levels of stress and having more severe, chronic anxiety. This can infringe on an individual's ability to carry out even the most basic, everyday responsibilities.

Just the thought of anxiety can make it difficult for some people to get through their day. The fear associated with having an anxiety or panic attack is generally enough to bring on an attack. There's a perpetual cycle of worrying that often accompanies anxiety and makes individuals feel inadequate and unable to control their thoughts or behaviors, despite knowing their thoughts are irrational and often worse than the situation warrants.

As someone who has managed a severe anxiety disorder for over 15 years, I can identify with the difficulties that chronic anxiety can present on a daily basis. Fatigue, sleep deprivation, difficulty focusing, heart palpitations, and trouble breathing are all common symptoms associated with chronic anxiety.

My disorder forced me to drop out of college on three separate occasions and was the catalyst having to close my first business.

Whether you are the CEO of a Fortune 500 company or the owner of a small retail business, chances are, one or more of your employees are suffering silently, and it could be costing you and your business a fortune.

Poor Performance

High levels of emotional and psychological exhaustion as a result of workplace anxiety can lead to a lack of focus and poor work performance. According to the Anxiety and Depression Association of America (ADAA), 56 percent of people who experience workplace anxiety report excessive fatigue, irritability, and feeling unmotivated. If left untreated, your employees will eventually need more time to complete their tasks, minimizing the amount of work they can adequately accomplish in a typical workday. This averages up to seven hours per week in lost productivity.

Providing your employees with an environment of empathetic supervisors and co-workers can lead to better quality relationships within the workplace, which can positively impact the effects of employee anxiety.

Excessive Time Off

Employee absenteeism and sick leave are all common business expenses. However, articles from the

National Center for Bio-Technology Information and the Natioanl Institute of Health point out that anxiety and depressive disorders are associated with increasing long-term work disability in comparison to other illnesses. It is reported that one in three absences are a direct result of anxiety and/or stress in the workplace. Please note that it is illegal to terminate an employee based on their disability or disorder without proper efforts to reasonably accommodate your employee's condition.

Although many businesses provide paid time off and sick leave, the long-term effects of too much time off can negatively impact the performance of your employees (see the "Poor Performance" section) and your bottom line.

Increased Health-Care Costs

The ADAA also reports that anxiety disorders cost the U.S. more than $42 billion annually, and those diagnosed are three to five times more likely to visit the doctor and more than six times more likely to be hospitalized as a result. With more than 40 percent of a company's earnings going to rising health-care costs, your company could expect to pay upward of $3,000 more per employee based on their anxiety alone.

Increased Turnover

Change is inevitable but can also be very expensive for your business. Employee turnover is a large contributor to your company's bottom line as it costs time, money, and productivity to replace an employee. With over 25 percent of employees reporting that their workplace is a major contributor to their stress and anxiety, the likelihood of your employees staying at their job long-term decreases significantly.

Stress and anxiety are often associated with more health complaints than any other complaint related to the workplace. Ensuring your employees feel supported and comfortable addressing their mental well-being with managers and co-workers is essential in increasing employee retention.

Low Employee Morale

Morale is a state of mind that affects confidence, productivity, and enthusiasm created within the framework of a company's structure. These factors also directly contribute to the four things I mentioned above. High morale is essential to a company's success, and although it's generally looked at as an intangible quality, it can have a damaging effect on the profits of the business.

Low morale in employees can often lead to withdrawn efforts and the development of counterproductive behaviors. Many anxiety sufferers report feeling judged and unsupported by their managers and co-workers, which only decreases morale and increases their wanting to find a new job. Encouraging open dialog between employees and managers as it pertains to the mental health of your employees can prevent their issues from being exacerbated.

When employees feel their employer is genuinely interested in their well-being, there tends to be an increase in productivity and retention, and this also lowers the company's expenses in recruiting costs and health care.

As a business owner, it's important to be informed, know the signs of employee anxiety, and provide your employees with the encouragement and support they need to manage their mental health. Corporate wellness programs are becoming increasingly popular and are specifically geared toward helping companies improve in all areas listed above.

Let's continue working to improve the culture of corporate America and learn to take care of each other in, and outside of, the workplace.

SIX THINGS YOU MUST DO TO EFFECTIVELY MANAGE REMOTE WORKERS

Tricia Sciortino

We've heard it all before. Remote workers are picking up steam at unprecedented levels. According to the U.S. Bureau of Labor Statistics, almost one-quarter of employed people perform some, or all, of their work from their kitchen table, home office, or back porch. And fewer business leaders question that virtual work promotes cost savings, ramps up performance, and deepens employee retention.

But, a major question remains: how can we onboard new offsite talent to ensure they stay the course, perform according to corporate values, produce as expected, and integrate well with other distributed team members? Perhaps some of these unresolved and persistent issues explain why companies like Honeywell and Charter Communications have banned work-from-home options. But there are many, many businesses starting out with a virtual model from Day One in addition to companies that have started to incorporate remote team members into their organizations. For these reasons, it's important to keep the conversation about virtual workplaces alive.

At BELAY, where I serve as COO, we have a number of full-timers who work from home, along with a multitude of contractors who do likewise across the U.S. As you might imagine, I've learned lots of lessons about hiring and holding on to remote teams over the years. And I know that early experiences and training can really make a difference.

Here's how:

1. *Aim for consistency—from Day One.* When all new employees are onboarding together, their introduction to the company begins from a basis of common understanding. And from this accord, they grow closer to the

business and to each other through the shared experience of orientation. New employee training can be delivered remotely, yet remain a collective process. Self-study programs, inclusive of videos, online communities, digital assessments, and more, give newcomers an opportunity to engage in content, communicate with others, and learn at the same time.

2. *Love technology.* Technology is a virtual company's best friend. We depend on it for security, cloud-based collaboration, daily communication, project management, and more. But, it's also the must-have in the toolbox for a company with remote employees. Not only do technologies support business needs, but they also enable visual communication, promote auditory engagement, and even allow for employees to test new skills, such as serving as presenters during online meetings and events.

3. *Know when to pick up the phone.* Virtual teams rely on technology and embrace its capabilities for connection, access, and collaboration. But one of the most important lessons I've learned is that back-and-forth emails mean the message— whatever it may be—is not getting through.

Someone needs to pick up the phone or get on a webcam meeting. Online dashboards and communication platforms have their place, for sure. However, old-fashioned talking cannot be replaced. Speaking with each other—and seeing one another, even if remotely—clarifies matters, prevents missteps, and resonates with so much of what still works for us as real people.

4. *Get together—regularly.* There's no absolute one-size-fits-all standard about how often teams should meet in person. But it helps to ingrain face-to-face gatherings into the operational DNA of an organization. At the very least, when the central, or corporate, players can convene on a routine basis, it helps to reinforce purpose and unity. If strategy and budget allow, it can only be beneficial to take this practice to the next level, creating ways for all team members to meet, greet, network, and learn together in the same physical space. This is especially true in the early days of their employment.

5. *Check in, with diligence and dedication.* It's important for new employees to maintain a connection to their managers and the broader

corporate mission. One way to foster and preserve this is through regularly occurring feedback. While impromptu check-ins can be beneficial, it's more intentional and meaningful to ensure performance meetings are a permanent fixture on HR's and supervisors' calendars. This can mean convening after the first 30 days, having weekly one-on-ones, and establishing other ways to assess expectations and performance by employee and employer alike.

6. *Learn from the same hymnals.* My company requires new employees to read the same three books. We selected these titles based on how well they reflect our corporate culture and align with our business personality. Sharing in this reading exercise sets the tone for how our team members should operate and perform on the job, while also providing them with new, relevant insights for their own personal and professional development, too.

Working remotely is no longer a new business trend or for the more cutting-edge companies. The latest technology has not only made it easy, but continues to advance the possibilities. To enhance your use of technology, it is essential that remote employees have the necessary tools and know how to use them. Training, tutorials, and support are integral so offsite employees do not feel lost or disconnected when they are five or 500 miles away.

It is important to recognize that, technology notwithstanding, the human element is still a factor and will hopefully remain as such. Actual phone conversations, get-togethers, and in-person meetings help humanize the business culture and unite those involved. Phone conversations should not become a lost art, nor should face-to-face discussions. Camaraderie, enthusiasm, and the team concept cannot be understated—even in a remote working environment.

The best way to work with remote employees is not to let them feel removed from the company.

THREE WAYS TO DECENTRALIZE MANAGEMENT AND BOOST PRODUCTIVITY

Dusty Wunderlich

Corporate structures are flattening. One big reason why is that the strict hierarchies of yesteryear are no longer effective for today's fast-paced, tech-driven industries. It is no surprise, then, that major companies are shaking up their management styles.

Take the example of Zappos. The shoe company famously runs as a holacracy in which employees self-organize instead of operating within a traditional bureaucratic structure. And consider that after CEO Richard Lepeu retired from his position at the Swiss luxury brand Richemont, the company eliminated the position altogether. Instead, the 20 "maisons" (the brands under Richemont) now report directly to the board of directors, distributing responsibility more evenly throughout that expansive organization.

Startups should take notice of this trend and embrace it. After all, new companies usually operate with constrained resources, always seeking ways to stretch their capital. And specialization is neither cost-effective nor likely to lead to the best early-stage products. Decentralization, however, encourages collaboration, efficiency, and speed.

Specialization is the Death of Early-Stage Innovation

Interdisciplinary integration enables startups to launch and grow quickly. Too often, entrepreneurs fail to build the right teams, which is one of the top reasons startups fail. Businesses falter, meanwhile, if they lack versatile employees willing and able to jump in wherever they see a need.

Highly specialized startups also do not go to market quickly. When only a handful of people in a company are qualified to work on product development, the business can launch just one project at a time. However, companies that hire multitalented employees develop MVPs faster, get to market sooner, and iterate on customer feedback before siloed startups have even held their first launch.

Strategic hiring, then, can ensure that a startup will use 100 percent of its resources all the time. My company got in on this trend early: rather than hiring a PR pro who deals strictly with media relations, we recruited a communications specialist who fits a variety of roles. A good rule of thumb for startups is that everyone should be able to do everything.

Ranch-Style Leadership

At our company, our culture has deep ties to our rural ranching roots in northern Nevada. That fact reflects on our work style as well. Ranchers after all are a self-sustaining bunch who use collective ingenuity to achieve their goals. Any one of them could change a truck tire or set a horse's broken leg.

This is the kind of interdisciplinary skill set we want our team members to embody, too.

In fact, this "ranch mentality" has driven our exponential growth because every one of our employees is comfortable taking initiative and working wherever needed. Most important, our employees understand their roles within the broader organization and how their work impacts our customers.

Don't get me wrong—even we have a loose hierarchy to ensure accountability for both ourselves and our clients. The key is breaking down the walls that keep departments and individuals from working together. When employees work in silos, they become disconnected from the customer experience, unless they're working on a customer service team. Software engineers, for example, will build the user interface for their companies' websites, but rarely do they understand how user interface impacts customer acquisition.

By facilitating collaboration between departments, such as engineering and marketing, employees understand how their work assignments fit together in service of their audiences. Startup leaders can use the following strategies to create decentralized businesses:

1. Rethink Structure

Forget about traditional hierarchies, especially in the early days. There may come a time when a more traditional approach works for an organization, but the startup stage is not it. Hierarchy-induced stress has long been linked to heart disease, among other health issues, and it increases voluntary turnover by 50 percent.

So, avoid these stress-related pitfalls; organize employees into autonomous squads that can work across disciplines.

Foster a sense of equality by encouraging conversations among staff members of all experience levels. My company practices department shadowing, in which founders and executives learn what people are doing throughout the organization.

When the concierge receives visits from the COO, and the vice president of marketing sits in with accounting, employees understand that we're all part of the same team, pursuing shared objectives.

2. Create a Team of "Intrapreneurs"

Startup employees make the best intrapreneurs because they're involved in so many areas of the business, they have unique views on what types of products will resonate with their markets. Google's intrapreneurship program, for example, empowers team members to pursue their ideas without getting approval from their bosses. They can partner with colleagues to explore concepts and potentially create new products for the company.

Cultivate a similar mentality by inviting employees to build new solutions and collaborate with their co-workers on ideas. Trust them to take initiative; don't require them to get a manager's green light before acting. Not only will this spur innovation, even as the company leaves the startup stage, but it will also inspire employee loyalty and enthusiasm.

3. Rally Around a Common Goal

Shared goals are a great way to bring people together and drive results. And while 75 percent of employers in one 2012 to 2013 survey by Queens University in Charlotte, North Carolina, rated collaboration as "very important," 39 percent of employees reported that their organizations didn't collaborate enough.

My own company decided to emphasize sales volume one year, and every department worked toward specific origination goals. Not only did each team's members want to perform the best, but they didn't want to let one another down. No one wanted to be the reason we fell short, so everyone worked harder to ensure we hit the target.

We also created opportunities for cross-collaboration, so different departments could gain insights into one another's processes as we pursued the goal. People work together best when they understand what's happening within each department and empathize with the unique constraints and pressures their colleagues experience.

A shared goal helped us foster more empathy and camaraderie between and among groups. We enjoyed our best sales year ever and saw an increase in proactive behavior throughout the company.

In sum, the flattened structure approach enables startups run on all cylinders at all times. Employees can burn out when working in silos because they feel that the success of a particular project falls on them alone. Alternately, flat teams share responsibilities and energize one another through collaboration. The personal, innovative nature of holacratic startups makes them more agile and better equipped to take on their markets.

ENTREPRENEUR VOICES SPOTLIGHT: INTERVIEW WITH RIAZ KHADEM

D r. Riaz Khadem is the founder and CEO of Infotrac, a U.S.-based consulting firm that specializes in aligning and transforming organizations. For the past 25 years, Dr. Khadem has worked as an organizational consultant in the areas of management and leadership. From his work, he has created a unique management model called Total Alignment, which he writes about in his book with Linda Khadem, *Total Alignment: Tools and Tactics for Streamlining Your Organization.* We talked to Dr. Khadem about his thoughts on improving production and addressing the value of managers.

Entrepreneur: What are your thoughts about improving productivity in the workplace?

Dr. Khadem: Productivity is an important topic. There are a lot of ways of improving productivity, such as training workers, automation, designing new processes for front-line workers, and so forth. What's missing is improving productivity among managers. For example, if you take an indicator, such as a KPI of sales dollars, and the numbers are good, that can reflect upon the value of the front-line sales team. Then you might ask yourself, "How do you measure the manager?" A sales manager will tell you that their added value is the total sales made by their team. While the team has displayed their value, the question is, "Did the manager do something to show his or her value in this scenario?" The manager may have added value by training the sales team, but the real value is being responsible for getting the team to exceed their sales quotas. If the salespeople were, for example, 120 percent over quota, this would mean the sales manager was spending more time with the best salespeople to improve their sales quotas. This is what good managers do; they find ways to make their teams perform better.

Entrepreneur: While this works well in smaller organizations, what happens in larger companies? Does it become harder to see the individual value of managers?

Dr. Khadem: If you think of the earlier example of the sales team and apply it to different levels of managers, at some levels, you won't find the unique indicator of their value at all. After all, you don't need three levels of managers all training or working closely with the sales team. When we take our clients through examples like this, it's a real ah-ha moment because they realize that if all these managers are not providing something of value, then you probably have too many managers at too many levels. This could mean you need to eliminate some of your managers and streamline the process.

Entrepreneur: Do you also find that too many levels of management, or too many managers, make it harder for the company to stay connected with their customers?

Dr. Khadem: Absolutely. What happens is that you lose alignment with the market, and decisions made at high levels are very disconnected from the customers who are dealing with employees many levels below. The lower-level employees know what the customer needs are, but those needs simply do not reach the higher-level executives.

Entrepreneur: Are there ways to keep the higher and lower levels of management both moving forward?

Dr. Khadem: Yes, another side of this coin is the fact that in many organizations, middle and upper levels of management are too involved, even frantic, about getting short-term results. They end up micromanaging and interfering with the people at lower levels. In our book, *Total Alignment*, we get the upper levels of management to focus on the future and the lower levels to focus on the current. By delegating the current concerns of the company to the lower level, it frees the upper levels of management to focus on the future of the company.

HOW WORKSPACE DESIGN CAN FACILITATE INCREASED PRODUCTIVITY

David Adams

Since the mid-2000s, the open-office layout has dominated design trends in American workplaces, thanks in large part to the unconventional offices of Silicon Valley tech giants Google and Facebook.

As office walls came down nationwide, business leaders discovered that the move not only opened up more space for equipment and staff, but also fostered conversation, collaboration, and team-building among employees. As of 2016, about 70 percent of U.S. offices use open workspaces.

However, recent studies have claimed that the open-office model causes employees more harm than good. Researchers argue that this type of work environment creates more disruptions and distractions, increases the spread of illness, generates more stress, decreases creativity and productivity, and results in lower employee morale.

The way I see it, office design, like everything in life, is not one-size-fits-all. The problems with the open office lie not in the concept, but in the limitations business leaders have placed upon it. That's why, even in the face of these negative reports, I stand by this modern workspace design—as long as business leaders provide the proper balance to make it work.

Zen and the Art of Workplace Design

Over the years, my company has experimented with various office designs, some being more successful than others. But overall, I've found that my team works best in an open-office setting.

Removing the physical barriers that once separated our employees has opened new levels of communication, idea-sharing, and problem-solving. And, yes, this layout has generated a greater sense of camaraderie among staffers working together toward a shared goal.

However, I recognize that some people simply need quiet or isolation to be their most productive selves. They just can't focus with so much movement and conversation around them, which is why I believe the "balanced workspace" trend is the office design of the future.

This design model calls for more variety in the workspaces within an open office, including secluded or low-disruption areas for those who need fewer distractions in their workdays.

One example of a well-balanced workplace is the New York City loft office of online investment company Betterment. Its multilevel office is largely open floor space, furnished with couches, work benches, tables, and even lounge chairs.

But the space also boasts closed-off sections, such as conference rooms for distraction-free meetings and "The Library," where noise must be kept to a minimum. This balanced layout has helped the company become an efficient startup in terms of productivity and morale.

Promoting Productivity Through Balance

Whether starting from scratch or modifying a work in progress, business leaders should evaluate the diverse needs of their employees, designing a space that offers a variety of areas from which to work. Here are a few design ideas to get you started:

1. *Create quiet zones.* While open offices are great for teamwork, they can generate a lot of noise. For employees who find noise bothersome, provide a quieter space away from the hustle and bustle of the shared work space. Set up a few couches in a corner of the main area with signage that discourages phone calls or talking. Or construct a few small, closed-off rooms at the edge of the office for important meetings or individualized work.

2. *Allow headphones in the office.* Personally, I love listening to music at work; it helps me focus and knock out any project on my plate. But to others, music is just another concentration-breaker. So, rather than play music over speakers at workstations or throughout the office, allow staff members to bring headphones to work. That way, they can either listen to music or enjoy the silence.

3. *Let the natural light flow.* Studies have shown that employees exposed to natural light during the workday are less stressed and less sleep-deprived than those who work

in windowless offices. That's another great benefit of choosing the open-office layout. When it comes to finding the best location or design for your open office, look for a place with a clear view of the outside world. Opting for big windows and lots of natural light will decrease employee stress and build a more productive, creative team.

4. *Think beyond the office chair*. Sitting from 9 to 5 every workday is truly terrible for you. In fact, it can bring on a whole host of health problems and even take years off your life. So, when designing an open-office space that encourages employees to mingle and collaborate, get creative with seating. Look into standing desks, yoga balls, lounge chairs, and treadmill desks. Or find other ways to encourage employees to interact and stay active, like game tables (foosball, ping-pong, pool, etc.), yoga time, or meditation breaks.

5. *Open your doors to new horizons*. Traveling has a big impact on creativity, and sending your employees on business trips has big psychological benefits. Adam Galinsky, a Columbia School of Business professor, is the author of several studies backing the

connection between travel and neuroplasticity. Look for opportunities to send your employees out into the world and break down the walls around your office building.

While the open-office design may have some flaws, it's not a lost cause. By recognizing the needs of a diverse work force and incorporating some distraction-free zones into your office, you can achieve a balance that promotes collaboration, boosts productivity, and keeps employees happy.

11

THREE UNIQUE PATHS TO IMPROVING OFFICE PRODUCTIVITY

Nathan Resnick

Being productive shouldn't mean you're chained to a cubicle. In fact, one of the biggest flaws managers make when evaluating employees is based on how long they spend at their desk. Similarly, there are other ways to make your workers more productive than by simply making them work more hours—research has shown things like group lunches increase productivity in the office.

If you're looking for out-of-the-box ways to increase office productivity, see three unique ideas below:

Provide In-Office Catering

Often, it's just easier to speak with someone over a meal, when you're more likely to feel comfortable. Besides, no one likes to eat alone. That is why all sorts of companies provide their employees with lunch and why companies like Hungry have started adjusting to the demand.

The link between in-office enjoyment and a solid lunch is strong. In fact, Hungry's cofounder, Eman Pahlavani said, "We're excited to launch an office lunch and catering service because Hungry can help boost workplace productivity, culture, and happiness."

You can also order from a popular eatery in your area. Of course, you want good food, but it's really about conversation and the camaraderie.

Buy a Ping-Pong Table

It goes against your intuition, but research has shown that office spaces with Ping-Pong tables create more effective teams. To the point, when's the last time you went to a startup's office and didn't see a Ping-Pong table?

To better understand an office dynamic with a Ping-Pong table, I asked Jack Richardson, a portfolio analyst at Square 1 Bank. During most of his working hours, Jack diligently reviews the ability of a company to pay back a loan. But when Jack has some downtime, he picks up a paddle to play Ping-Pong. His office has set up a Ping-Pong tournament that has weekly rankings. This, as he notes, boosts morale across his team and increases his alertness.

Provide Outdoor Educational Perks

Nowadays, having a corporate gym membership program is normal, but you can still set your company apart by giving your employees the chance—and incentive—to learn new outdoor skills.

As an example, Dizzle, a San Diego-based startup that builds mobile real estate apps, offers its employees a monthly stipend to try new outdoors activities. So far, employees have learned to sail, rock climb, and mountain bike. This boosts team outlook and builds stronger relationships among employees . . . especially when they're learning together.

The old school idea of nose to the grindstone and chained to your desk doesn't really facilitate better results from workers. With tech companies leading the way, many of the more culturally enlightened businesses are recognizing the value of enthusiastic employees who get a break from the daily grind to mentally refuel, much as you stop to refuel your car. With so many people juggling a host of responsibilities, clearing the mind once a day can be akin to pushing the reboot button and watching your computer's speed improve.

Managers may also be best served by getting a feel for what would best improve office productivity. Not every office wants a Ping-Pong table. Gather some suggestions, and if possible, mix it up a little. Have yoga on Wednesdays, and pizza parties on Fridays. For the old-school naysayers, consider the value on having employees who look forward to coming to work rather than those looking at their watches and updating their resumes often. Which do you think will be more efficient? The main point here is that an entrepreneur doesn't necessarily have to work harder or longer to be more productive. Balance is important, and an office that promotes teamwork is one that promotes productivity.

WHY YOU CAN'T AFFORD TO FIXATE ON RESULTS AT ANY COST

Mike Canarelli

If you've been in the business world for any period of time, you've likely heard someone say, "Results matter." And they do, yet focusing only on results can be a recipe for disaster.

When results are all that matter, people will do whatever it takes to achieve them. That's just one of the problems with the Results Only Work Environment, otherwise known as ROWE.

What Is ROWE?

ROWE is a management strategy that pays employees for the results they deliver rather than the hours they work. The model traces its origins to 2003, when enterprising human resources executives Jody Thompson and Cali Ressler floated the idea to the retailer Best Buy. The electronics giant became the first major corporation to implement the strategy. Clothing retailer The Gap soon followed suit. Since then, hundreds of businesses, large and small, have adapted ROWE to fit their specific industries and organizations.

ROWE, along with coworking, telecommuting, and flex time, is intended to empower workers through autonomy. The mission is to co-create a happier, hungrier, and more effective work force.

In many cases, ROWEs deliver the results intended. Employees feel a greater responsibility and no longer think of their positions as jobs. Instead, they identify with it as a career. Likewise, ROWE itself often is successful. Teams operate more efficiently and typically perform well.

What's the downside? There are issues with ROWE and very real ones.

Trust and Accountability

If you've assembled the right team, trust and accountability are a given. But complete freedom affects people differently. Getting a project done on time and under budget can be stressful, and the pressure only builds as expectations grow greater. Even good people can resort to cutting corners or dabbling in unethical behavior as a way to continue delivering results.

Communication

In environments where collaboration or frequent communication is necessary, it may not be enough to Skype or text remotely. Sometimes, walking across the room and asking a quick question can solve an immediate pressing problem. Communication in a ROWE can be complicated and messy—especially if teams or team members are on different schedules.

Transitioning

Some employees don't do well in a ROWE. Employees transitioning from a traditional workplace may find the new rules confusing or threatening. Even for those embracing the idea, wrinkles can turn into creases with mixed messages, unclear directives, or results that are moving targets.

If the workplace allows executives to work remotely but requires customer service team members to keep standard hours, the ROWE also may need to address issues of jealousy and resentment. For a ROWE to work, everyone at every level needs to buy in. It's a major culture shift. In many cases, well-liked staff might need to be let go if they fail to keep up. This can have a deleterious effect on the team's morale.

Managing

Investing in your staff is an important building block for any business, and that means occasionally holding team-building exercises or company trips. In other words, it's more than just delegating. Managers in traditional workplace environments are part coach, part motivator, and part director. In a ROWE, managing is essentially boiled down to organizing. Unfortunately, this can prohibit growth.

Results

If results are the only focus, what happens if those results are poor? Live by results; die by results.

Best Buy's stock valuation peaked in 2006 but then tumbled steadily downward. In 2012, Best Buy hired new CEO Hubert Joly. He took a hard look at the company and its declining numbers. A year after taking the helm, Joly abandoned the ROWE strategy. The effect on the stock price was immediate. By the end of the year, Best Buy shares soared more than 28 points, from $11.67 per share on December 21, 2012, to $40.17 per share on December 27, 2013. Best Buy has enjoyed considerable success after reverting back to a standard 40-hour workweek.

Although many leaders who have switched from a traditional workplace extol the virtues of the ROWE, this type of management strategy probably works best when it's incorporated into corporate culture from the beginning. Before you embark on the road to ROWE, be sure to take a top-down look at your operation. Ask whether ROWE really is the right fit for you, your team, and your clients or customers.

The answer could surprise you.

It's also worth noting that ROWE is better suited for some industries than others. In retail sales, factories, hospitality, hospitals/medical, education, and other businesses in which there are specific hours to deal with customers or an ongoing need to meet customer demand as it is deemed necessary, this strategy is less likely to be effective. If tasks are location specific and visible, it is unlikely that you can use ROWE.

In other situations in which teamwork is essential, there is also a less likely opportunity to enact ROWE effectively. However, knowledge-based industries in which work is performed "behind the scenes," such as marketing, advertising, accounting, or engineering are more likely to have success with ROWE. As with most things today, there are also the hybrids—companies that have found ROWE works in one department of the company, while not in others. For example, the advertising and marketing department may be able to work autonomously on projects, while the customer service department will need to be available as needed by customers. Many companies have tried ROWE in one or two departments to determine whether it is right for them or not.

PART II
MANAGING PRODUCTIVITY— REFLECTIONS

From quiet zones to headphones, there are a host of ways in which managers can improve the efficiency and productivity of their work force. The key to such success is centered on the idea that it's no longer about expecting people to simply tow the line. Instead, it's all about giving them a reason to want to come to work or work harder from a remote location.

The progressive manager wants to meet company goals while focusing on the numbers and embracing the changing office culture and dynamics. Physical spacing is also changing, with walls giving way to more open settings in an effort to bring people together. Hierarchical settings are also being transformed and flattened, and both fitness and fun are becoming part of the work experience because all work and no play . . . well, you get the point.

Of course, managers still need to know that their people are getting their jobs done. With the rapid rise of off-site employees, this means maintaining a strong connection to those working in various locales and making sure no one who is off-site feels left out.

Clearly, managers have a lot on their plates today, as their responsibilities increase with technology and the desire to get the most
out of more savvy employees.

MANAGING EMPLOYEE PERFORMANCE

B ecoming a manager does not mean that you suddenly excel at evaluating the performance of others or giving feedback. But it does mean you are in a position to do so. Many critics are adept at providing reviews, but most are based on their personal opinion and not necessarily what their customers, clients, or (if you're a film critic) movie-goers want to see.

Employee evaluation begins by understanding the job of each employee as it fits into the company's plans and goals. It is not about how much someone stays out of your hair or bothers you. It is not about someone doing your work for you or a great job at tasks that are otherwise designed to make you look good—this is addressing the ego-centric managers in the crowd. It is also not about your need for perfection.

Employees will make mistakes. As a manager, you need to accept that as a fact of life—people make mistakes. The question is: how do you deal with them? Are people learning from them or inventing a variety of excuses, such as the dog ate my sales report?

People not only learn from mistakes, but they also learn from bad experiences and managers. So, rest assured, if you micromanage, berate employees, and set them on the fast track to employment elsewhere, if nothing else, you will have taught them a valuable lesson in what not to do should they move on to management.

Being able to provide effective feedback is a hallmark of successful manager-employee relationships. Exactly how much transparency and honesty you are able to express yourself with will vary depending on the personalities of those involved. Can you provide straightforward feedback and have difficult conversations with people? Hopefully, yes. Can you pound them into the ground with brutal honesty? Sure, but then you will be seen as a bully. The point is that there is a fine line between what is for people's own good, or the good of the business, and what is simply taking out your own frustration on others. Managers have to fall in the right category.

Feedback is very important since without it, people have no idea if they are on track or veering off on a tangential path. Praise and appreciation are also very important. As a manager, one of your goals should be to learn how to walk that fine line and to give effective feedback and praise as well. As Mary Poppins said, "A spoonful of sugar makes the medicine go down." In business, you might say a spoonful of praise makes the feedback go down. Hey, it worked for Mary Poppins.

In the upcoming chapters, you will see what can be learned from bad bosses, what radical candor means, the fine art of acknowledging mistakes, and about providing feedback.

TEN FOUNDERS SHARE WHAT THEIR WORST BOSS TAUGHT THEM

Nina Zipkin

We've all had bosses that make us crazy—whether it was a supervisor with a big temper, one that watched your every move, or the one that never knew what he wanted. But even if at the time it was frustrating or demoralizing, there is an upside: you'll never catch yourself being that kind of manager.

We caught up with ten successful entrepreneurs who shared with us the lessons they learned from the worst bosses they've ever had.

Daniella Yacobovsky, BaubleBar

One of the things I have learned is to communicate openly and honestly with the folks you work with. Try to understand where their requests and feedback are coming from, and be open to their feedback. When you're first starting and you're a small company, it's definitely easier to do. As you grow and have more people, it is a harder thing to scale, but that doesn't take away the importance.

Gavin Armstrong, Lucky Iron Fish

People who are bullies act that way because they are insecure about something else. They are very demeaning and not appreciative.

You want to be very respectful of the people working with you. Remember they work with you, not for you. Be complimentary of their work because they are putting a lot of time and effort into it.

Merrill Stubbs, Food52

Being indirect about what you want or what you expect is a really terrible tactic for managing people. It makes them feel like the ground is shifting beneath them—that's an impediment and distraction from people doing their best work.

Melissa Ben-Ishay, Baked by Melissa

The importance of open communication. When I think of the worst boss I ever had, I don't think of just one person.

I didn't have a mentor. I didn't have someone who wanted me to succeed. I didn't have someone who took the time to sit down, have a conversation with me, and help me be better at my job. So now, I really make the effort to be clear and honest with my employees and sit down with them and communicate.

Oliver Kharraz, Zocdoc

I learned to only make promises that I can keep. I remember how upset I was when promises were made to me that were not kept, and I promised myself that I wouldn't do that.

Jennie Ripps, Owl's Brew

I learned how important it is to engage with my own team and ensure that there is buy-in across the board at an individual level.

Tim Chen, NerdWallet

Ego gets in the way of success. I worked at a hedge fund that had a real *Lord of the Flies* feeling. It was pretty crazy. The problem with ego is the best ideas don't win because you have trouble facing the truth.

Kyle Hill, HomeHero

The worst boss I had was actually a soccer coach I had in high school. I wouldn't say he was a bad coach, but he yelled at me a lot. I realized that was something I could not handle. So, my dad ended up pulling me from the team. I didn't understand it at the time. I thought it wasn't a big deal, and I had tough skin.

But my dad was adamant about this. He said, "I don't want people talking down to you because it hurts your self-confidence. I need you to have the highest self-confidence going into in everything you do in life; otherwise, you're not going to want to do it."

I think it lends itself to being treated with respect and dignity. My dad said, "You can be stern, you can bench my son, you can take him aside and tell him what he needs to improve on. But don't publicly reprimand him."

Even to this day, I tell people, "If you're upset with me, whether it's my co-founder or an employee, talk to me like an adult."

Bastian Lehmann, Postmates

One thing I try to do is help the people that want to do more. I want to help them realize that when they are at Postmates.

The worst boss I ever had told me that I couldn't do that. He was weak and afraid someone was hungrier than him. When I saw someone trying hard and they gave it everything they had, that boss would not give them guidance and help them succeed.

Heidi Zak, ThirdLove

The one thing I've noticed from having different types of bosses is that the best ones have a clearly articulated vision of what the team is working toward. You have to communicate it effectively and do it often. That's what I try to do; you can't say it too often.

14

FIVE TOUCH POINTS TO BOOST RETENTION THROUGH TRAINING

Sam Bahreini

Retention is crucial to the success of any company. Unfortunately, it's difficult for retail employers to reduce their turnover. The best way to improve retention rates is investing in employees and their professional development.

Learnkit's 2015 report titled "Creating a Win-Win-Win Learning Strategy for Your Organization" found that 89 percent of the 421 employees surveyed feel it's important their employers support their learning and development. With most employees craving growth, why aren't companies stepping up their development game?

Let's take a look at how retail employers can improve their retention by focusing on training their employees throughout the employee lifecycle.

Hiring

It all starts here—finding top talent and sending out offers. It's best to base hiring entry-level employees on their attitude and on the degree to which they share company values. This way, employers know new hires are engaged in their work for more than just a paycheck. It's then up to employers to educate their candidates on what the company stands for.

First of all, promote core values to candidates on the careers page and relevant social media accounts. Then, start sharing employee testimonials that describe how current staff members put these values into action.

The main challenge is translating abstract terms and phrases into action, and that's why it's crucial to get job descriptions just right. Integrate core values into the postings, and show what kinds of behaviors reflect them.

For example, if the company values growth and innovation, describe a behavior that would reflect that, like an employee who actively seeks learning opportunities and jumps in when new responsibilities present themselves. To screen for this, ask behavior-based interview questions so candidates share past experiences to prove they act according to their employer's values.

Training

This is arguably one of the most common pain points for retail companies. A 2015 infographic from the "State of Employee Training" survey conducted by West Unified Communication Services found that one-third of the 200 full-time employees surveyed said current training programs aren't productive, while another one-third replied that the material is not interesting or engaging.

The simple fact is that one-size-fits-all onboarding sets new hires up for failure. They want more than boring slideshows and packets of paper.

Break up training into modules that cater to the role and emphasize the big picture. For example, when training sales reps, give them some context on why the company values honesty and how customer satisfaction retains customers and improves sales. Make the training interesting and engaging by using games, integrating educational programs and applications, and role playing.

Coaching

Training should get new hires off their feet and onto the floor. It's on the frontlines that they learn the most because supervisors and management can focus on coaching them in real time. This is where creative role playing comes in.

With creative role playing, employers can coach new hires on how to interact and react in hypothetical situations. They should enlist the help of current employees to present common scenarios. Not only does this help new hires learn, but it also acts as a great tool for team building.

Role playing creates a safe place to show new hires how to deal with conflict resolution and improve their communication skills. Start introducing them to common situations where they need to apply those specific actions and behaviors they learned from the training guidelines, and observe to see how they perform.

Mentoring

After onboarding, connect new hires with more experienced employees. Mentors help them build communication and customer service skills in real time. They can also empower new hires with constructive feedback and recognize them when they succeed.

New technologies include introducing video into the mix to help managers capture and assess performance. These video solutions are perfect for companies that want to establish an employee recognition program where they can review how employees perform and then offer an incentive or reward for the A players.

Employee recognition helps engage employees and keep them motivated. Make sure to celebrate each employee equally with a focus on new hires.

Succeeding

Create a succession structure with assistant managers and department supervisors to ensure that when a manager leaves, there is a smooth transition. Don't get caught off-guard and have to scramble for replacements.

With a strong training program, companies are more equipped to boost retention and build a talent pipeline. This way, when higher-ups vacate, there are plenty of qualified employees ready to jump in and take over.

Integrating technology into employee sourcing and talent management is the best way for organizations to stay relevant and to prepare for the future of the retail industry. When companies invest in their staff's professional development, employees want to stay and grow.

15

WHY RADICAL CANDOR IS THE FEEDBACK METHOD YOUR STARTUP NEEDS

Emily Muhoberac

Honesty is key when it comes to feedback. But many leaders are inhibiting growth by not being honest enough with their employees.

What does true honesty look like? In 2017, a spokesperson for online clothing retailer Thread shared with BuzzFeed an example of the typical feedback an employee might receive from the CEO, which reads: "We often have moments in conversations where you quickly say your point, then stop abruptly and look at me nervously, bracing yourself and trying to perceive my reaction. It makes me feel uncomfortable. It makes you seem less confident."

This type of blunt feedback has a name: radical candor. While many entrepreneurs shudder at the thought of being so straightforward with their employees, radical candor has proved to be successful at startups like Thread.

This process works because young companies don't have the time or resources to play games when it comes to office politics or passive-aggressive approaches. And because expectations change so frequently in startups, employees need to have a clear idea of what's expected.

Honest feedback also keeps employees engaged. A 2014 survey from Officevibe shows that 98 percent of employees aren't engaged in their work when they don't receive feedback. Radical candor helps keep employees on track so companies can grow.

How Radical Candor Can Jump-Start Growth

The most valuable asset entrepreneurs have is their people, so it's important to make the most of them. At Sapper Consulting, our team consists of people with varied backgrounds and experiences, and some of our best ideas have come from our "green" employees.

Radical candor helps these young and inexperienced employees grow much faster—it allows managers to correct problematic behaviors immediately. This, in turn, allows B players to grow into A players and A players to become all-stars. Even all-stars have room for improvement, and radical candor allows every employee to reach their full potential.

Employees also trust their team members more because they know if there's something they can be doing better, someone will tell them—no more wondering where they stand or if they're being kept in the dark. Our company's employees are given the autonomy to make their own decisions because they know someone will inform them if they're not doing their jobs properly.

While radical candor helps employees grow and gain trust, it can also be used to help leaders "fire fast." When managers and employees are honest about feedback, it doesn't take long for leaders to determine good cultural fits and bad ones.

Radical candor can have a profound effect on productivity and growth, but it needs to be implemented the right way to avoid negative results:

1. Have the Right Intent

Implemented the wrong way, radical candor can quickly transform into bullying in the workplace. Radical candor is about truly investing in other employees to help them improve—not complaining about or making fun of people. After an employee receives feedback, she should feel like the other person was trying to help her improve and not trying berate her.

It's also possible to be gentle while being honest. For example, a manager could approach an employee and say, "I'd like to try to understand why you've been consistently turning work in late." The goal is to open up a dialogue to get to the root of the problem without being hurtful.

Kim Scott, the cofounder of Candor Inc., explained in a blog post for First Round Capital that Sheryl Sandberg, her boss at the time, helped spark the idea after Scott gave a presentation to the executive team at Google.

After Scott finished her presentation, Sandberg mentioned to her that she used many filler words (such as "um") while speaking. At first, Scott brushed it off, thinking it wasn't a big deal. But then Sandberg said to her, "When you say 'um' every third word, it makes you sound stupid." Scott took notice and realized she had room for improvement.

2. Make It a Habit

Giving feedback needs to become a habit. Don't wait until monthly or quarterly meetings to address issues; address them as quickly as possible.

However, it's important to always give negative feedback in private—never in front of a group. Whenever I see an opportunity for feedback, I pull that person aside and discuss it with them. This gives employees the chance to make immediate improvements rather than letting them keep repeating mistakes until they're corrected in a quarterly meeting.

In addition, employees who don't receive continuous feedback often feel nervous when it's time for reviews. When employees are used to receiving feedback on a regular basis, it feels normal and doesn't induce anxiety.

Employees who regularly receive feedback are also more likely to be engaged in their work. According to 2014 research from Officevibe, 43 percent of employees who are engaged in their work receive feedback at least once a week. That leads to happier employees and increased company growth.

3. Include Everyone

In a radical candor system, everyone's on a level playing field. The CEO should be able to receive feedback from an entry-level employee, and the executive team shouldn't be held to a different standard than everyone else. We ask all our new hires to give feedback to the CEO or executive team during their first week on the job. That way, they'll understand the culture and feel more comfortable giving and receiving feedback.

Executives also need to be open to feedback in order for the radical candor system to be effective. Career company Levo and career expert Vicki Salemi discussed this topic with Millennials to learn more about how lower-level employees interact with bosses. One accounting employee shared her story about how she discussed her working style with her manager.

She said she sat down with her manager to figure out a way the two could communicate more clearly, and he was very receptive to her ideas; he wanted to make the learning process as efficient as possible. This type of open dialogue between employees and managers not only eases workplace relationships, but it also increases efficiency.

4. Keep It Specific and Actionable

Only give feedback that is helpful and can lead to change. For example, rather than saying, "You're constantly late for meetings," say, "I've noticed you're consistently late for meetings. I've found that reviewing my schedule first thing every morning has helped me stay organized, and it may help you as well."

Positive feedback should also be specific: A simple, "Great job today" doesn't sound as sincere as, "You did a great job leading our meeting today."

All employees (even the all-stars) have room for improvement, and a combination of positive and negative feedback helps employees grow—in fact, 72 percent of employees said their performances would improve with helpful feedback from their managers, according to a 2014 survey from *Harvard Business Review*.

Growth is critical for startups, and it all begins with feedback. Radical candor is a global phenomenon in the startup world, and it can lead to a more trusting and collaborative work environment (and tremendous company growth).

ENTREPRENEUR VOICES SPOTLIGHT: INTERVIEW WITH CHUNG-MAN TAM

Chung-Man Tam joined Homesuite as the new CEO in May 2017 after cofounding Qwilt software, serving as Chief Product Officer at Chartboost, and spending the past six years working with Startup Helper, providing his knowledge of leadership and management to startups. The San Francisco-based Tam is now in the unique position of leading a new business in a rather new niche market. We talked to Tam about getting the culture in place while strengthening communication and creating an inclusive work environment.

Entrepreneur: As a new CEO, what do you look at first from a management perspective?

Chung-Man Tam: As CEO, you want to know where the company is headed from a strategic perspective and from a market perspective. You also want to have a quantitative measure of what success looks like and line up each of your team members so they can direct the things they are doing day-to-day with the goals you are looking to achieve.

As for managers, we want to make sure they are getting people to focus on what it is they are trying to do together. But what is so important is that you want to get everyone excited about it. You want them to figure out how the world is going to be better if you're doing all these things. You're looking for ways to empower teams and have managers that understand how to make choices, prioritize, and make the right decisions that lead to the greater goal.

Entrepreneur: How do you and your managers handle employee and customer feedback?

Chung-Man Tam: At the end of the day, we're trying to deliver from a customer perspective what we call a five-star experience. When we talk to our landlords and building managers, we want them to have a five-star experience as well. Therefore, we want our managers and our employees to think about what they can to today and tomorrow to create that five-star experience. We talk about it and give them the opportunity to be introspective, take their heads out of the day-to-day, and think about what we want to achieve. This allows people to provide good feedback and fresh ideas.

I set aside time to touch base with people who don't report to me directly so I can hear how they are doing. I want to get their feedback on what we could be doing better as a company and what I could be doing better in my job. I also communicate with managers and ask how their team is doing and who they have talked to this week. I want them to learn from their team, and I want to learn from everybody in the business. Bottom-up feedback provides everyone with a chance to be involved in the growth of the business.

Entrepreneur: How do you touch base regularly and effectively with your managers to make sure you are on the same page?

Chung-Man Tam: We do so in a couple of different ways— we have quarterly meetings to discuss the bigger, broader things and how we're going to measure the success of the projects they and their teams will be working on. I work with them on setting the right level of difficulty, and then, we re-evaluate on a monthly basis. We look at how we're doing in terms of reaching our goals and decide whether there are any that we need to change. On a daily basis, I'm looking for folks that are asking questions about how things are going—it's important for the managers to learn to become the leaders that they are. That means having the room to make mistakes and learn from them, as well as having the confidence to make important decisions.

16

FIVE REASONS EMPLOYEES SHOULDN'T FEAR MAKING MISTAKES

Rehan Ijaz

We live in a culture where mistakes are to be avoided at all costs. Often, when we make an error, it creates feelings of embarrassment, frustration, or even fear, especially when it happens at work. There's nothing like a missed deadline or even an unfortunate typo to cause anxiety, especially when you work for a perfectionist who has little or no tolerance for human error.

While there are certainly places where there is no margin for error, such as in the finance department, where a single transposed digit can change everything, for the rest of us, a mistake isn't the end of the world. In fact, when it's acknowledged, corrected, and analyzed, a mistake can actually help improve performance and increase innovation. So, why do so many managers expect perfection?

Mistake Prevention Isn't Job No. 1

As a leader, you understand that everyone is looking to you for guidance and that your superiors are looking to your department for performance. You know that if your department doesn't meet its goals and live up to standards, then you aren't proving your value as a leader—and that could lead to serious consequences for your career.

If you are like many leaders, you take this responsibility seriously—so seriously, in fact, that you make it your personal mission to prevent any of your team members from making mistakes. It's your job to save people from themselves and ensure that they do everything correctly, right? Wrong. That type of approach to leadership only leads to micromanagement, a failure to delegate, and a sense of fear and lack of innovation within your team. Who wants to take a chance on doing something creative or risky when failure will lead to disappointment and a lecture from the boss?

It's important for leaders to realize that instead of discouraging mistakes and making employees feel so boxed in that they are reluctant to take risks, they should actually be encouraging and celebrating mistakes. In fact, management guru Peter Drucker actually once suggested that companies seek out people who never make mistakes and fire them because if someone never makes a mistake, they never do anything interesting. Whether or not you follow Drucker's advice, the idea is that risk takers make mistakes, but you need to take some risks to succeed. Telling employees that they cannot fail and punishing mistakes is not going to move your business forward.

Why Mistakes Are Important

Obviously, you don't want to create a free-for-all environment where people are careless with their work and there is never any accountability. However, by supporting a culture that doesn't penalize people for the occasional error, you can enjoy several key benefits:

1. *A more honest and open environment*. When mistakes aren't a big deal, your employees will spend less time trying to cover them up

and more time fixing them. It's much easier to say, "I screwed up, here's why, and here's how I plan to fix it," than it is to scramble to cover the mistake. Being forthright allows for a more trustworthy and open environment.

2. *A more positive learning culture.* Allowing mistakes gives your employees the freedom to admit what they don't know—and then find ways to improve their knowledge. As a leader, you could help create formal training and development programs that allow employees to improve themselves and your company. Instead of trying to fake their way through tasks and hoping for the best, being able to admit shortcomings and getting support to develop and grow helps improve employee satisfaction and loyalty and improves your work force.

3. *A more innovative team.* The most common reason that people aren't innovative or creative is that they fear failure. Give your team space to fail, and watch the innovative ideas start to flow.

4. *Fewer mistakes.* When you are worried about making a mistake, what do you do? If you're like most people, you are so focused on being

perfect that you overlook small things or get so nervous that you make more mistakes. Allowing a margin for error helps reduce that stress while also reducing the likelihood of mistakes happening in the first place. This is because your team isn't under pressure to be perfect.

5. *A happier team*. Finally, removing the punitive aspect of making a mistake helps improve employee satisfaction. You'll enjoy a more positive relationship with your team and see more collaboration and trust.

Again, there are times when there is no margin for error and perfection needs to be a priority. Those times are few and far between. Creating a culture that allows for experimentation, exploration, and yes, errors is going to make you a stronger leader and, more than likely, help you reach your goals and prove your value to the company.

THREE LEADERS WHO TAKE EMPLOYEE APPRECIATION TO THE NEXT LEVEL

Rose Leadem

Forget about office perks—today, many bosses motivate their employees with vacations and holidays gifts. That's right, bosses are dropping big bucks on things such as cruises, cars, even weddings. It's no wonder these companies are surpassing their sales goals.

From the small-town boss who took his 800 employees on a Caribbean cruise to the CEO who pays for his employees' weddings and children's college tuitions, check out these three bosses who take employee appreciation to the next level.

Iowa Boss Takes 800 Employees on a Cruise

When the freezing temperatures of winter were approaching, employees at Waterloo, Iowa-based Bertch Cabinet won't have to worry—they're headed to the Caribbean. After meeting their yearly sales goals, the company's president Gary Bertch promised to take his 800 employees on a week-long cruise down south.

This isn't the first time Bertch has offered vacation incentives. In 1989, the organization began taking companywide cruises, but that perk vanished after 2005 when sales began to stagger.

"We just tried to get all our people pumped up a little more to achieve the various goals, both customer-oriented goals and financial goals," Bertch told the Waterloo-Cedar Falls Courier. Apparently, the plan worked!

CEO Promises to Pay for Employee Weddings

Major life events don't run cheap. That's why this CEO wanted to alleviate at least one financial stress from his employees: weddings. Upon his discovery that one of his employees was working double shifts with an ill mother at home just to cover upcoming wedding expenses, online grocery store Boxed CEO Chieh Huang decided this was no way to live.

He not only offered to pay for this employee's wedding, but he announced to all his employees in his Edison, New Jersey, warehouse that he will pay for all employees' future weddings. Huang is no stranger to helping out his employees, whom he considers family. Not long ago, Huang announced that he will pay for his employees' children's college tuitions, too.

Founder Gifts Employees' Apartments, Cars, and Jewelry

Jewelry tycoon and owner of Hare Krishna Exports, Savji Dholakia wants to make sure all employees are taken care of. That's why he gifted 1,260 cars and 400 apartments to his employees as Diwali gifts (the Hindu festival of lights) in October 2016.

"Our aim is that each employee must have his own home and car in the next five years," he said.

The cars and apartments come in recognition of great performance and dedication from employees over the past five years. And this isn't the first time Dholakia has made an effort to provide employees with homes and transportation—in fact, he's been awarding employees like this since 2012.

Of course, these are unique situations and far from your everyday perks, but business owners and managers need to think about how valuable their employees really are to their success and the success of the company. Too many owners and managers are so busy looking at sales figures and an endless stream of metrics that they lose sight of success when they see it.

And they lose sight of the people who helped them reach that success. While affording weddings, cars, and houses may be more than the budget will allow, there are slightly less pricey perks that can be used to entice employees to excel at their jobs and show their dedication to the company. Weekend getaways, tuition for employees who want to return to school, or free enrollment in a health club can start the ball rolling when it comes to giving something to say thank you to your employees. In the case of New Belgium Brewing Co. in Colorado, for example, they brought everyone together to follow their lead as an eco-friendly, green, sustainable company. While unifying for a good cause, they also bought everyone in the company bicycles to ride to and from work.

Be creative, and as the company grows, let the perks for your people grow, too. Look at generosity as something that will pay off, as well as make you feel good about yourself.

FIVE TIPS FOR GIVING FEEDBACK TO CREATIVE PEOPLE

Will Meier

It doesn't matter if you hire the most talented, creative minds in the world—internal or external—at some point, you'll have to give them feedback. And that's where things can get dicey. Giving great feedback is an art in itself. But giving great feedback on creative work is really hard to do. You have to be specific without being overbearing. You have to guide the project without manhandling it. Make no mistake: bad feedback can poison a project faster than almost anything else. The feedback you give—and the way you give it—can be the difference between a project everyone loves and a project everyone wishes had never started in the first place.

Don't panic. Here are five ways to improve the way you give good feedback.

1. Always Go Back to the Goal

One of the hardest parts of giving feedback is figuring out where to start. Most feedback is a mixture of emotions, personal taste, and critical thinking. This makes it just as difficult for the person receiving the feedback as it is for the person giving it.

Luckily, designers Adam Connor and Aaron Irizarry lay out a very helpful framework for thinking through feedback in their book *Discussing Design*. Forcing yourself to answer these four questions is a great starting point for getting your head around what's wrong—and what's right—with a design (or a film or a tagline or anything, really).

- *Question 1*: What is the objective of the design?

- *Question 2*: What elements of the design are related to the objective?

- *Question 3*: Are those elements effective in achieving the objective?

- *Question 4*: Why or why not?

Using this framework will help you take yourself, your emotions, and your biases out of the equation so you can focus on giving feedback that is objective, goal-oriented, and—most importantly—useful. As a bonus, these questions are also a great way of making sure you understand the goals of the project. If you have a hard time answering Question 1, then there's a good chance the project is about to come off the rails.

2. Don't Count On "Knowing It When You See It"

"I'll know it when I see it," is code for, "I have no idea what I want." This often leads to a situation where a creative is just guessing at what will make a client happy, rather than thinking critically about the ultimate goals of the project. It's a terrible place to be as a creative—especially for a freelancer on the outside of an organization—and it's a terrible place to be as a client. The remedy to this problem is twofold: 1) Go into the project with a very clear picture of what you want and why you want it. Find inspiration online that you can share. Understand what you like about the example and why. Then, 2) realize that the final product will never be exactly what you had in mind. Often, it will actually be better if you're willing to see it.

3. Be Specific

Intuition doesn't come with a vocabulary. Where a lot of feedback goes wrong is in the misinterpretation of jargon. What does "fresh" mean? What makes something "visceral"? Often, it can seem like you and your creative colleague are on the same page, only to find out in the next round of revisions that you're on completely different planets. But even without the proper vernacular, you can find ways of getting specific about what it is you're feeling/seeing/ wanting. Include examples of what you're talking about. If you want something to feel fresh, include a design that feels fresh to you, or be specific about what in the design doesn't feel fresh. If you want snarky copy, show 'em some snark. Make sure you share sources of inspiration, your influences, and the things you like. Remove the guesswork, and don't let jargon get in the way of clarifying what you want. Include Google image links.

4. Take Time to Give Good Notes

Creatives put a lot of time and more than a little heart into the work they deliver to you. So, it can be very discouraging for them to receive feedback that feels dashed off, untimely, and thoughtless—even if that feedback is, in itself, very good. In the now classic book, *Creativity, Inc.*, Pixar cofounder and president Ed Catmull reveals Pixar's standard for a "good note." Our team at Musicbed has found this is a great litmus test for any piece of feedback you give. Here's Ed:

"A good note says what is wrong, what is missing, what isn't clear, what makes no sense. A good note is offered at a timely moment, not too late to fix the problem. A good note doesn't make demands; it doesn't even have to include a proposed fix . . . . Most of all, though, a good note is specific. 'I'm writhing with boredom,' is not a good note."

Don't rush your notes. Don't dash something off. You don't have to have the solution (in fact, it's often better if you leave that to the creative). Just start a productive conversation. The time you take to make sure your feedback meets the requirements above will be rewarded.

5. Be Quick to Praise

A little bit of praise goes a long way. Creatives will always do better work for people and projects they care about. So, be sure to communicate what you like about a piece, what you appreciate about what they are bringing to the project. Hearing what's working can be as informative as hearing what isn't. Give them something to hang their hat on, something that makes them take pride and ownership in the project, rather than begrudgingly trudging through your long list of changes. Empower your creative colleagues to bring their talent to the table. Isn't that why you hired them in the first place?

It should not take great effort to force yourself through the arduous process of giving good feedback. It takes a positive approach. Nonetheless, many people are jaded. But trust me, giving good feedback is worth it. Not only because you'll get a better product in the end, but because working through the process of giving good feedback will sharpen your skills as a marketer, a communicator, a business owner—a person, basically. Before you shoot off a confusing, discouraging feedback, remind yourself why you care about the project in the first place. Remind yourself what your colleague brings to the table. Stay positive and your enthusiasm will transfer to your team. And believe me, you're all going to need it by round 11.

PART III
MANAGING EMPLOYEE PERFORMANCE—REFLECTIONS

They say, "learn from the best," which is good advice, but you can also learn from the worst. As we saw in Chapter 13, business founders remembered, and learned from, the worst bosses they ever had. The truth is that people tend to remember the best and the worst and not all that much in-between. Once you leave a company, you will likely remember your best and worst clients, perhaps your best and worst evaluations, and your best and worst managers but not much else.

People also learn through mistakes, which is why managers should not make an issue out of them. Most mistakes are minor, and making a big deal out of every error creates an environment that stifles creativity and creates a fearful work environment that will have people hiding work rather than handing it in. Instead, some companies even discuss mistakes at meetings and let people explain how they corrected them and what they learned from them.

Perhaps the most significant factor in managing performance is giving feedback. There is an art to offering feedback, and many managers fail to master it until they have been on the job for a number of years. What makes feedback so difficult is that to do it effectively, you need to be honest, critical, supportive, and positive all in the same scenario. And, as Will Meier pointed out in Chapter 18, it's always good to be quick to praise.

Of course, you also need to find the right time and place to engage in feedback, which is probably the biggest mistake managers make. Talking to someone in private rather than in front of a group of their peers is essential.

It's also important to remember that positive feedback is just as important as negative. The manager who has nothing to say until someone does something wrong is not providing a balanced or fair appraisal of that employee's work. It's not uncommon to hear people explain that their boss never says much of anything to them unless they have something to criticize. As a manager, you should avoid focusing only on the negatives because you will lose the enthusiasm and productivity of your employees. People want to hear that they are doing well, especially the creative folks, as noted in Chapter 18, who may not always be measured precisely by numbers or metrics.

Since giving feedback is not always easy, here are some questions to ask yourself when doing so:

- Do I provide constructive feedback or only point out what the person did wrong?

- Do I assume that the individual had a positive intent or sound accusatory?

- Should I be specific in my feedback or general?

- Should I be critical about their work ideas, or do I criticize the individual?

MANAGING TEAM DYNAMICS

Team dynamics refer to the chemistry between team members that influences their decisions and actions as a single entity. Managers need to watch how the dynamics of the team unfold and determine how they can best steer the team in a productive direction. They need to be mindful that the psychological makeup of the individuals on the team and the relationships that develop within can create positive or negative team dynamics.

Such dynamics can play a major role in the management style and culture of the business. Conversely, the culture of the business, which is the combination of numerous factors, can play a role in team dynamics. In the right environment, team dynamics can be greatly enhanced.

After all, managing culture as it relates to how you manage your team, is all about the people, how they interact, and how much they enjoy their employment. People who are more enthusiastic and feel a sense of belonging to the workplace community have more incentive to work harder and show more diligence. This can greatly boost team dynamics.

As a manager, you want people to be "turned on" about working in your company. In fact, as leadership coach Ben Simonton says, "Turned on people figure out how to beat the competition; turned off people only complain about being beaten by the competition."

Building a strong team dynamic means hiring the right people, not only for their skills, but also for their ability to be team players and thrive in a diverse workplace. It also means as a manager, you need to build bridges between employees, whether that means common interests at break time, multigenerational team building, regular evaluations, or enhancing the overall understanding of diversity in the workplace. Of course, there is an organic aspect to that dynamic and culture that emerges from the characteristics and personalities of the people who work in a company.

In the upcoming chapters, we explore a variety of aspects relating to business culture and creating a harmonious work environment for your employees. As Steven R. Covey says, "Always treat your employees as you would treat your best customers."

19

FIVE TIPS FOR DEALING BETTER WITH WORKPLACE DIVERSITY

Chidike Samuelson

Diversity is a good thing. Always has been. Always will be. But, still, it can be just as dangerous as it is good. While a diverse staff can be a great thing and bring amazing new perspectives to the table, it can also cause palpable tensions that destroy whatever benefits have already been brought to the table.

The reason is obvious: people are touchy about issues like race, religion, politics, and personal orientation; yet understanding "diversity" can help you become a better manager and employer. Here are a few tips.

1. Recognize the Many Types of Diversity

As already stated, diversity has many categories, and not all are readily noticeable. To notice them, you have to peer a little deeper. One key reason many people feel comfortable in one workplace, but unfulfilled in another, may be because they are diverse in those subtle little ways.

That all your staff hail from the same state doesn't mean they are not diverse. For instance, you will be aware of the obvious diversities, such as race, religion, and gender, but you also need to find out about the guy who always slinks away from birthday celebrations; you need to notice the diversity of thought among your staff members.

The meaning of diversity has changed. Factors can be as simple as height or age. People may, rightfully or wrongfully, feel that they are singled out, or treated differently, because they are shorter or taller—21 or 61. As an astute manager, you need to pay attention to how people feel they are being treated, especially if an uncomfortable situation arises. Be careful, however, not to jump the gun and assume how someone will react.

2. Redefine Discrimination, and Clamp Down on All Its Forms

In a friend's company, where most of the staff worked remotely and hailed from diverse nations, "Hello Jimmy, how is Africa?" addressed to a man named Jimmy, who actually was working remotely from Africa, degenerated to a racist slur when voiced repeatedly.

Discrimination is the most common result when people are uncomfortable with diversity and the reason that workplace diversity can be harmful at times. The Workforce Diversity Network has redefined discrimination to include actions both intentional and unintentional, conscious and subconscious—all of which should be recognized and acted on by the manager closest in contact with the offending staffer.

3. Celebrate Diversity in All Ways Possible

Nikos Antoniades, CEO of easyMarkets, was asked in a 2016 interview, shortly after he took that job, how he handled diversity.

"Our clients are based in over 160 countries around the world," Antoniades replied. "I love the unique perspectives brought to the table, and I particularly enjoy the many celebrations we have—including the Chinese Moon Festival, Polish National [Independence] Day, and our Brits this year [who] celebrated Pancake Day. Recently, we celebrated Carnival, which kicked off with a barbeque at work and was followed by a week of dressing up in costumes. Most of the celebrations are around food—who can complain?"

Moving out of your comfort zone to other people's once in a while is a surefire way of maintaining decorum in a diverse workplace.

4. Keep Reaching Out

Keep trying to learn about your staff, especially the new hires. Talk to them personally, and find out where they are from.

Vincent Seglior, who was the World Trade Institute's director of international training for 12 years, advises in a 2012 blog post that managers should place new hires who are from a different culture under longer-term staff who are from similar backgrounds but have become more integrated.

It's necessary to maintain the company culture, but to do this, you may have to hold an orientation session any time there are personnel changes in your department. Be a manager who develops open relationships with your diverse staff. Talk to them positively—both in a group and individually.

According to Seglior, if you remain curious about, receptive to, and open to learning about people's different cultures, your staff will benefit, and so will you. But, remember: there is a difference between curiosity and prying. People from all over the world want to be respected and as such not singled out as "the guy from Nigeria" or "the woman from Belgium."

5. Don't Assume People Understand Your Jokes

Workplace jokes are often what make work fun, and the resulting camaraderie is what makes people look forward to coming to work the next day or to the next online meeting. Yet, certain jokes and comments must be carefully censored.

A former manager I know made a joke in a staff meeting about people who didn't go through college. I understood that he was trying to be funny, and it really would have been funny had there not been a fair number of people among the staff who hadn't gone through college. I saw their faces turn red, literally, and the manager didn't even notice.

Not everyone has your experience or privileges. You need to know your staff well and be sensitive to their differences. Don't assume they ought to get your joke because the next time you pass them over for a promotion, they may think it's because of their differences.

That being said, a diverse work force creates differences and some challenges, but if handled well, it can explode with benefits.

20

HIRING BRILLIANT JERKS CAN COST YOU THE CULTURE THAT BROUGHT SUCCESS

Nicholas Wagner

Growth is important, but so is culture. Hyper-growth in a dynamic industry is a good problem to have, but even a "good" problem needs solving. A 2015 article, "It's Better to Avoid a Toxic Employee Than Hire a Superstar" from *Harvard Business Review* (HBR) explains that "avoiding a toxic employee" can save a company a great deal of money—even more than the company would make by hiring a star performer. But double- or triple-digit growth rates put recruiters under pressure to hire quickly without bringing problematic employees into the fold. So how do you accomplish finding the right hire quickly?

Ad tech hit a speed bump over the last year or so as venture capital investors have pulled back slightly. However, the sector as a whole continues to grow as more ad spending shifts to digital. The segment's overall revenues are expected to triple by 2020 to $100 billion. That growth, and the programmatic space in particular, attracts a set of workers who are understandably interested in joining an industry with a strong future. Yet when it comes to readily usable programmatic skills, it's a sellers' market.

It's the Personality, Stupid

That's why ad tech recruiters frequently find staffing an issue. Factor in a generally fresher ecosystem with shorter tenure and quicker job rotations than in more traditional industries—energy, banking, or retail—and you find yourself hiring younger or less experienced candidates than you normally would.

Younger, less-experienced candidates offer many benefits, including agility, fluency with the most recent tech trends, and comfort with the world as it is (or is about to be). However, experience-based assessment (i.e., assessing what they will do based on what they did) is less useful when candidates draw from a shallower well of experiences. You may find yourself interviewing a person who has only a single internship to talk about. Predicting how such a person will behave in a full-time job is tricky. Sometimes, you'll offer a complex problem to learn how they might approach it, and they'll talk about how they decided to study in Barcelona rather than London. I can't count the number of candidates who responded by telling me me how they decided to break up with (or stay with) their girlfriend or boyfriend. So, you have to work with what they give you. How are they tackling a challenge? Any challenge?

Weeding Out Brilliant Jerks

You need to make sure that each new hire will commit to the company's vision and will quickly sync with the rest of the team. That requires knowing your company's ethos and culture. If the new hire's commitment is unclear, invest some time to make it clear.

One thing we (and now, Arianna Huffington and Uber) look to avoid is hiring the "brilliant jerk"—a person who is bright and capable but unpleasant. Some companies enjoy hiring brilliant jerks because it fits with a competitive internal environment. But at many firms, as the HBR article referenced above notes, such hires cause a great deal of damage.

Short of asking, "Are you a jerk?" and hoping for an honest reply, there are a few questions that can suss out such tendencies. One is asking, "Tell me about somebody great." The answer will demonstrate whether someone can be passionate, animated, and admiring of others.

You can see if they speak from the heart. If they don't, you'll get a better feel for what sets their gears in motion. Do they seem to view others as stooges, praising those who tell them what they want to hear, or do they let others shine?

You want someone who can explain their expertise in a way that's approachable. If they can't, their skills are likely to stop with them. At the same time, look for indicators of a person's mindset. If something fails, rather than looking for ways to make it better the next time, they look for someone to blame. That's a no-go.

Trust in Consensus

No one should enter a company after fewer than four interviews, and they should first meet all the key people they will work with. Everyone needs to agree that the person will be a good hire. Those requirements are a service to the prospective hire as well as to the company.

Some will argue that such a process takes too long. Rigorous criteria can lead you to leave a position open for months rather than filling it with the wrong employee. Make sure you have a scheduling ninja or two so you don't lose qualified applicants to excessive delay.

The C-suite needs to understand that the quality of workers determines a company's culture, reputation, and productivity. This is especially true in a fast-growing company in a fast-growing industry. It can be tough to hire methodically when supervisors are begging for help. Thoughtless hiring, though, can undo years of hard work. No one wants that.

Take your time.

TEN WAYS BOSSES WHO MAKE NICE BRING OUT THE BEST IN THEIR EMPLOYEES

Sherry Gray

Leaders do not have to be mean to be effective. Authoritarians tend to think that by being soft they will reduce their staff's respect and motivation. Steve Jobs, for example, was famous for being mean, critical, and tyrannical to his employees.

But successful leaders are rarely like Steve Jobs. He's the exception that proves the rule. Studies show that overly rough bosses spawn motivational problems with their staff. The stress of working under a mean boss can negatively affect employee health.

A 2015 study at the University of London discovered a significant link between cardiovascular disease and management-induced stress. Researchers at the University of Concordia found that when employees think of themselves as highly stressed, their health insurance costs skyrocket by nearly 50 percent. The Institute of Naval Medicine found that a hard-core management style drives away the best talent, leaving behind only those who perform at a lower level. And conclusively, Esprit de Corps ran a poll that indicated most employees would rather have a nicer boss than receive a substantial pay raise.

The bottom line: People leave bad bosses—not bad jobs.

A considerate boss boosts cohesiveness and productivity, and leaders perceived as compassionate motivate their subordinates to be more helpful to colleagues and more committed to their teams.

Here are ten ways in which the boss "making nice" pays off:

1. *Let them know where you stand.* Mastering the art of kindness takes commitment and determination. But it's worth it. Real

kindness is shown in straightforward and direct interaction with employees, so they know where they stand and why. You don't have to pull your punches to be kind. When someone knows you're genuinely concerned about them, they are willing to listen to your input—both positive and negative.

Outplacement data compiled in 2016 by Mullin International over the previous three years shows 60 percent of departing employees will remain in their former company's eco-system as buyers, suppliers, influencers, or competitors. Treating your employees well pays off in multiple ways even if they aren't with you anymore.

2. *Strong doesn't have to be harsh.* Leadership means strength but not harshness. A soft answer turns away wrath and keeps employees better balanced. When your staff sees that you can maintain poise and self-control, even under the most difficult and demanding situations, they are more willing to follow your lead and make their own sacrifices for the good of the team or department or company. A smart boss does not jump in to take control at the first sign of trouble. They guide workers to work

out their challenges in a way that is not confrontational.

3. *Confidence is not arrogance.* Confidence, like measles, is contagious. Employees want to be around a confident boss but shun the company of a know-it-all. The best way to show confidence is to show competence that you really know what you're talking about. And then, if you really don't know something, confess it and find the employee/team member who does know about it and learn from them.

Great leaders are humble. They don't put up artificial barriers between themselves and their employees. Their door is always open, and they don't require others to do things they can't or won't do themselves.

4. *Be positive, not delusional.* To remain positive yet keep your feet on the ground and your head out of the clouds is a remarkable skill that not every manager or supervisor can master. It takes some trust in others to follow through and enough confidence in your own abilities to remain unperturbed when the you-know-what hits the fan. And it will. It always does. So, don't just say the

glass is half full; instead, get your employees to see that the glass needs a lot more that only they can provide.

5. *Teach—don't preach.* The corporate world is full of people who believe they should do unto others before others do it unto them. A great boss is one that makes the time to instruct employees in their duties and responsibilities but is not stingy with praise. Chewing out an employee for anything, whether it's a bad habit or careless work, leaves a bad taste in everybody's mouth.

6. *Grin and bear it.* Your team will back you up just as far as they feel that you will back them up. So, go for broke. Show them that you'll "take a bullet" for them. It's not an easy thing to do, but if you're prepared to do it when the occasion arises, you can be sure they will have your back from then on—and that's a wonderful feeling for any boss to have.

7. *Strive for balance.* Employment isn't a birthday party, where everybody gets cake and ice cream and plays games all day. But neither should it be slavery in a salt mine, with the whip always cracking. There's a balance—a delicate one that bosses have to maintain

between a fun work environment and a productive work environment. Sometimes, it has to be fine-tuned down to each individual. But your people should always be aware that you're striving to make things pleasant for them, while still expecting them to meet their goals.

8. *Be personal but not intimate.* Find out about your staff's family and hobbies and ambitions outside the office. Remember birthdays and anniversaries. Show concern when there's a health crisis with an employee or someone close to them. Let them talk about their pets. But when the talk turns to romance or finance, that's when the wise and kind boss quickly finds somewhere else to be. Quickly. Show you care, but stay out of the drama.

9. *Provide fearless feedback.* Feedback can be either positive or negative. Find opportunities to discover your workers doing something right, and praise them for it. When you have to deliver negative feedback, always end the conversation by sincerely asking, "What can I do to help?" A boss is not doing an employee any favors by procrastinating when it comes to giving negative feedback. Get it over with,

and ask the golden question. The solution can start that much sooner.

10. *Sharing is caring.* A great boss will share credit. Ladle out sincere praise like gravy. Sincerely enjoy the success of their subordinates. Kindness is never about you—it's always about the other person. Live for others, and your own life, at work and at home, will prosper.

WHY A "LIVING AND BREATHING" COMPANY CULTURE ISN'T ALWAYS A GOOD THING

Jayson DeMers

If you've been plugged into the entrepreneurial world at all in the past decade or so, you've probably heard people describe how they want all their employees to "live and breathe" the company culture. The metaphor here is designed to imply a deep commitment to that culture—usually defined as its values, character, and priorities.

Company culture is a commitment so deep that it can no longer be distinguished from employees' own individual values, character, and priorities.

It's also an interesting vision, and one that certainly has its merits. When all your employees are so deeply committed to the company, they'll be willing to work harder for their shared goals and more likely to work together. They'll also contribute more positively to the overall environment, creating an accelerated feedback loop that makes the culture even stronger.

However, a "living and breathing" company culture takes the idea of culture to an extreme that yields more than a handful of downsides, and the only reason the concept exists is because of our arguably temporary obsession with the importance of company culture.

The Rise of Company Culture

Organizational culture has been a concept in business and management since at least the 1970s, but it's only recently that "corporate culture" has become a buzzword. You could argue that this is so because more business leaders are discovering the true objective value of a positive company culture; I'd argue, however, that it's something closer to a fad.

Company culture started to accelerate in popularity once people started realizing that many tech startups in the Silicon Valley region—which turned into multibillion-dollar juggernauts—all had surprising cultural features in common that broke from traditional office environments.

Obscure furniture, casual dress codes, and a youthful energy were, and still are, stereotypically common features in this context, and they fuel a false association. Specifically, both culture and financial success differentiate these companies, so surely, the two factors must be connected.

The end result is a still-growing obsession with creating a unique and "modern" corporate culture— one that employees must be "living and breathing" to allow for that culture's full benefits.

How Company Culture Can Go Too Far

This illustration shouldn't convince you that corporate culture is bad or unnecessary; in fact, I'd still argue that it's critical for a business' success. But we should be careful not to overestimate culture's benefits and should avoid shoving it down workers' throats.

Company culture can go too far in at least the following ways:

- *Homogeneity*. Some of the best ideas in the world are the ones you didn't see coming. They come from outside sources and outside perspectives or arise from uncomfortable situations. Accordingly, having a diverse environment, with many different minds and perspectives, is important to the survival of a business. Being too rigid and too serious about your company culture encourages a kind of homogeneity; if all your employees think and act alike, they'll all solve problems the same way, which will limit your growth and put you at risk for bigger problems down the road.

- *Stress and pressure*. Using the phrase "living and breathing" company culture implies that working for this company is as important as life itself. While some people thrive in high-pressure environments, chronic stress isn't good for anybody. If you make your workers feel like nothing matters except their work, eventually they will begin to suffer lower morale and display lowered productivity.

- *Polarization*. Approaching company culture with this extreme level will also polarize your newest hires and job candidates. It's true that you'll naturally attract some people who already fall in line with your company values, but you'll also scare away some serious talent who may differ with you on a handful of key points. Is that scenario really worth it?

- *Misplaced values.* Don't forget that this is still a business and your bottom line is profitability. Company culture is a useful way to make your workers happier and more productive, but the "living and breathing" angle can sometimes interfere with that vision. For example, if an employee's deviation from your cultural norms ends up earning better results for your business, you shouldn't complain or reprimand the employee.

- *Cult vibes.* Finally, to a more subjective point, enforcing your company culture too strictly or seriously gives off some serious cult vibes. This is off-putting to employees, clients, and customers alike—so try not to turn your brand into a corporate brainwashing scheme.

Finding the Right Balance

Remember that company culture is still important, and your employees should fit, to some degree, into that culture. The key is to find the balance between nurturing that culture and mandating it. It's different for every business; depending on your size, your niche, and your personal preferences, you may end up settling on one end of the spectrum or the other.

There isn't a single right answer, but you owe it to your staff and the future of your business to give it some serious analysis.

ENTREPRENEUR VOICES SPOTLIGHT: INTERVIEW WITH GLENN LLOPIS

Glenn Llopis is the chairman of the Glenn Llopis Group, a nationally recognized thought-leadership, human capital, and business strategy consulting firm. As a speaker, consultant, and executive coach to Fortune 500 companies and beyond, Glenn guides leaders and organizations to embrace a new type of thinking that helps them evolve and stay ahead of the rapid changes in the workplace and marketplace to drive growth. He is the bestselling author of the books *The Innovation Mentality* and *Earning Serendipity* and a contributing writer for *Forbes*, *Huffington Post*, and *Harvard Business Review*.

Raised in a Cuban-American household, Glenn notes that there is something to be said for the immigrant perspective. "I have created a whole methodology around it, which I call the *Innovation Mentality*," which also just happens to be the title of his latest book from Entrepreneur Press.

We asked Glenn about today's workplace dynamics and corporate culture.

Entrepreneur: What are your thoughts on creating an inclusive company culture, and how have they changed over the years?

Llopis: It's really interesting because if we go back about 15 years, or perhaps a little longer, the state of business was one where there weren't a lot of options. Competition had that box-store mentality. You knew who the market leaders were across the major industries. The economy was strong, companies were managing growth, and when you manage growth, you become wired to operate as if you're just taking orders. There was predictability and consistency, so management was basically making sure we were accountable to do what we had to do without disrupting any form of momentum that we had created. Management was more prescriptive: you did five things, and you would get the same five outcomes. We just had to be more efficient than ever before to keep the momentum going. The culture was one in which people felt that they were contributing to an organization, but it was very much prescribed by the business. In other words, the individual didn't have to do much beyond following the templates.

Today, it's a different dynamic because we're in a time in which we are no longer managing growth, but instead, we're trying to find a way to create it or recreate it. As a result, we need to create an environment in which the individual has to have greater influence. Managers and leaders can no longer follow a template because the market is moving so fast, there is so much more competition, and companies just don't have all the answers.

Creating, or recreating, growth requires a whole new set of skills and competence that needs to come from the individuals. Those that touch the business have to influence more than they've ever had to before, and because people are doing much more than their job titles, it's become very difficult for companies to build a culture people can buy into and trust. Today, there are more cultural and generational shifts, and people no longer want to be managed by a template. They want to be managed by managers who exhibit trust, transparency, and vulnerability, knowing that if the company is going to grow, individuals will have greater influence.

Entrepreneur: Since managers can't just be prescriptive, because things are changing around them and they are not yet familiar with managing growth, are they caught in the middle?

Llopis: They are. In many organizations, they have a choice to evolve, but often, management is not evolving fast enough. There is still an inability to engage with their leaders and with their employees in a way that helps the organization understand how they are going to define the future.

Entrepreneur: Are managers not coming into their jobs prepared for this new type of management?

Llopis: What I see out there are so many people who are promoted to management roles because they are good at sales, which doesn't mean they are good managers. They're not taking enough time to recognize what people aspire to be, and as a consequence, people are not reaching their full potential. I would say that because of ineffective management, today people are operating at 40 percent of their full potential. In an environment to drive sales, sales, sales, we have created this culture that is so execution-minded that people aren't sharing, and when management doesn't encourage people to share or be innovative, they don't care as much or trust as much.

Entrepreneur: What is your methodology to moving managers into this new environment—from prescriptive to inclusive?

Llopis: You have to be able to see opportunities in everything. You have to create an environment to allow people to get out of their comfort zones and into new ways of doing things. You have to allow people to anticipate the unexpected. When you're in an execution mindset, you're always just doing what you're told to do within the box that you're given, but because the market is moving so fast, you have to be able to give people the room to explore. People have to have a sense of purpose, and even if they are not actually entrepreneurs, they need the freedom to have that entrepreneurial spirit.

23

SIX GENERATIONS IN THE WORKPLACE (AND WHY WE NEED THEM ALL)

Marian Salzman

Every night, I turn on the news and hear how we are more divided than ever. But when I enter my office each morning, I walk past five generations of colleagues—all working together with remarkable levels of collaboration and focus, each bringing the insights and expertise unique to their individual experiences while also representative of their generation.

As a trend spotter, I see this as a new reality, empowering brands and businesses smart enough to recognize and leverage it. With a wider breadth of talent in the work force than ever, companies have access to an incredible array of skills and knowledge, which is great news. As the business landscape continues to accelerate, we will need them all.

But that doesn't mean organizations have a handle on managing this diversity, much less leveraging it for competitive advantage. Suffice to say: this is no time for a set-it-and-forget-it management style. Understanding the attributes of each generation will help organizations harness their different styles and insights to engage the ever-widening audience of their brands.

Employees born in the 1940s came of age in the 1950s and early '60s—at a time of organizational hierarchies and monolithic media. Many managers mistakenly assume they are frozen in that mindset. These are highly skilled employees— not mastodons! They have a tremendous ability to understand complex structures and objectives, an ear for sweeping, emotionally connecting narratives that unite rather than divide, and an admirable ability to not sweat the small stuff.

Employees born in the 1950s were shaped by intense innovation, from the postwar space race to Beatlemania to the civil rights, antiwar, and women's movements. They know the value not only of structure but also of rebelling against it. They have a knack for being able to question authority and, simultaneously, be authoritative. This is a great gift in an age where brand narratives have to convince, engage, and innovate.

Employees born in the 1960s formed their earliest memories during the time when cultural traumas like assassinations, protests, war, impeachment, and riots shook the nuclear family. They experienced the rise of everything from disco, punk, and hip-hop; to hippies, preppies, and yuppies; to the drug culture and the war on drugs. This group gets the promise, excitement, and power of participation and transformation on a more personal level. They have respect for sustained effort and the rebelliousness to know when and how to shake things up.

Employees born in the 1970s—the grouchy pragmatists of Generation X—got invited to the party after everyone left and then were asked to clean up. The least sentimental, they are also the most resourceful. They bring a healthy dose of skepticism and a results-focused appreciation of what works. Gen Xers went to college before email and the internet but adapted quickly, pulling themselves out of the dire job market of the early 1990s and sparking the dotcom boom. When it went bust, it reinforced their cynicism while strengthening their sense of possibility. They are level-headed managers.

Employees born in the 1980s—aka Millennials— have been terribly maligned. The stereotypes about managing them are too tired to repeat and largely untrue. Many experienced 9/11 in their early teens and entered the work force at the height of the financial crisis. And I am here to tell you: thank goodness they arrived when they did. We desperately needed their hyper-connected, open-minded, and almost surreally confident energy to help move us forward. They have an intuitive facility for connection; a second-nature command of digital, mobile, and social; and a healthy aversion to cumbersome structures.

Employees born in the 1990s—Generation Z—are now starting their careers. Like their grandparents, with whom they are often close, they have come of age in a time of war as the norm and a sluggish rebound from a financial crisis. They see digital as a tool (professional and social) to facilitate connection, often more in the real world than on social media. Empathetic and accepting, they are natural collaborators and realistic about challenges.

Gen Zers represent some of the best of each previous generation—but they are, of course, very young and need the guidance and insights that all those generations can offer.

Embracing the skills, the spirit, and the various mindsets that each generation brings to a business provides a wealth of sources from which to get ideas, some that are ripe for recycling, and others that are yet to be tried. There are so many possibilities with a cross-generational staff.

More often than not, however, teams tend to focus on their peer groups and, unfortunately, lose the value of such cross-generational diversity. Writing off everyone over the age of 40 as "ancient" is a big mistake, as is disqualifying the newcomers just out of college as "kids." The manager who can bring together experience, old-school work ethics, and values with wide-eyed enthusiasm and tech-savvy confidence can create a team broader in scope than a single-generation team. The single-generation team may come up short when branding the business to other generations of potential customers. Just thinking about the strengths of each makes me excited for the possibilities of multigenerational mentorship and collaboration. If I could build a six-member dream team for communications today that could quickly implement and adapt to all the facets of agile PR, I couldn't do better than one member from each generation. Lucky for everybody, they are all already here—and prepared to collaborate.

CREATING SPACE FOR INTROVERTS TO FLEX THEIR SUPERPOWER

Pratik Dholakiya

In the business world, we've all heard and read classic euphemisms which imply that success is directly tied to the quality of being extroverted. In fact, facets like high performance and business potential are directly (and stereotypically) attributed to this quality.

But introverts have their own contributions to make. These people are characteristically defined as shy, quiet, passive, or antisocial (though those qualities may not be unilaterally true for every introvert you employ). And these personality attributes make introverts highly adept at strategic planning, creative thinking, and problem-solving—skills that are an asset to any team.

Of course, as the company leader, you have to know how to enable those skills. And that requires a leadership and organizational approach that provides accommodation without objectifying or singling out an introverted individual. From the socializing that goes on in your office space to the dynamic that emerges at team meetings, your managers can potentially impact employee retention for the better by adopting a tailored approach to your introverted staff.

Identifying Introverts in the Workplace

The scale of introversion is not always about extremes; an individual may have many extroverted tendencies but still identify internally as an introvert. This can make it rather difficult for managers to identify members of the team who have different needs to help them perform to expectations.

Psychometric testing is a cornerstone of recruitment and human resource management and is a reliable method of determining the degree of introversion and best practices for a balanced team environment.

Tip

The Myers Briggs Personality Inventory is also a valuable resource for managers and human resource professionals, and can provide essential management insights.

Open Work Spaces

Globally, there exists a trend that is being driven more by economics and less by employee need: the open-office layout. As commercial business space becomes more expensive, and as businesses grow, moving to a larger building may not be a practical solution. Enter options that help make the most of existing workspaces: telecommuting and the open-office plan.

The problem is that open-office layouts do not work for many introverts. Characteristically, these employees are pensive, deep thinkers who require a place that is quiet and free of stimulation and distractions to provide their best work. Open offices hinder concentration by eliminating that private buffer, and in these settings, noise becomes a problem that prevents introverts from focusing effectively.

In terms of team dynamics, open-office settings also inhibit the development of close personal relationships between introverts and their colleagues. Uncomfortable with conversations that are audible by "everyone around them," introverts are likely to avoid personal conversations during the workday. They'll avoid those brief, friendly interactions that enhance communication among co-workers because those interchanges lack the privacy and sense of safety for having a conversation.

Introverts have a lower tolerance to excessive stimuli (which distracts and creates stress for them), and they prefer face-to-face engagements with smaller groups of people.

Tip

Moving to an open-work-space plan may be inevitable, but creating "withdrawal space" for work is essential to productivity (and retention). Ensure that you incorporate small pods or offices that can be used by individual staff who wish to retreat to a quiet area.

Feedback

Part of any small departmental or large organizational meeting is the prompt to share feedback and ideas. The first people to speak up naturally are extroverted members of your team, who feel more than comfortable being heard in front of a crowd. Extroverts are also better able to process criticism in front of others, which makes them virtually fearless about sharing ideas, comments, or problems with their team.

The average introvert, meanwhile, may be frustrated in a public feedback situation. As the deep thinkers in your organization, introverted personnel are not short on ideas or suggestions for creative problem-solving. However, if the only opportunity that is provided occurs within a very public setting, you can count on your introverted staff to avoid sharing. Not only will an organization miss the value of their contributions, but introverts may feel diminished in value and excluded from the team.

Tip

Extroverts tend to dominate most meetings, and while their enthusiasm and contributions are important, it is equally important that leadership professionals moderate that engagement to prevent other members from feeling overwhelmed.

At the end of any small or large meeting, ensure that you offer a method for introverts to submit their feedback, comments, or ideas in writing. This gesture can be as simple as encouraging staff who did not have an opportunity to share to send a summary email with their questions, comments, or ideas. Being open to contribution by a variety of methods helps introverts feel less overshadowed by more outspoken colleagues.

Body Language and Work Preferences

It's easy to determine in most cases how extroverts are feeling about a situation, considering these people exhibit expressive body language and visual cues. Introverts, however, can demonstrate a flat affect that may be misinterpreted by both management and extroverted team members.

An introvert, for example, may require more time to formulate an idea because of their personality style. However, many studies have demonstrated that more than 70 percent of individuals with high-functioning intellects are introverted.

The additional time that an employee takes to articulate a response or to provide an idea is frequently the precursor to innovation. It is not a lack of responsiveness but rather an intense ability to handle complex issues and provide results. Given the time to matriculate and organize their ideas, introverts provide highly detailed plans and solutions.

Tip

Team-building exercises and personality sensitivity training can be valuable ways to increase awareness and combat stereotypes and assumptions. By identifying both extroverts and introverts as a performance asset, both groups can work cohesively (and respectfully) within your organization.

Negative Feedback

In some research studies, it's been reported that extroverts are adept at managing public criticism far better than introverts. While introversion is not synonymous with shyness or weakness (despite stereotypes), these people find the spotlight to be a stressful place to be in social and professional settings. An extrovert may, therefore, be able to process a reprimand in front of other colleagues and recover quickly, while an introvert may experience significant stress and personal offense from the same feedback.

Tip

For important feedback or performance-review meetings, managers (whenever possible) should communicate privately with introverted colleagues or employees. Not only will this eliminate a deeply humiliating experience for the introvert, but it will also allow them the safety and reassurance to respond to questions.

Organizations that understand the ways in which both personality types offer value and those that are willing to pivot leadership approaches, depending on whether an employee is an extrovert or introvert, can anticipate a more harmonious environment, increased employee engagement, and long-term retention of talented professionals.

DOES YOUR COMPANY CULTURE MATCH YOUR BRAND?

Marty Fukuda

A 2017 article, "Thinx Promised a Feminist Utopia to Everyone but Its Employees," published by Racked, takes a hard look at Thinx and the company's inability to deliver the same type of culture to its employees as it does its consumers. Specifically, the piece says Thinx's goal to create "a feminist utopia for everyone" fell short when it came to the most important audience: its team.

The challenges of building a thriving workplace environment while at the same time growing a business are daunting, but it can be done. Here are four ways to ensure that your employee culture is as strong as you advertise it to be.

1. Create and Review a Company Culture Deck

A culture deck is, simply put, a series of slides that outlines how your team behaves. It can be a list of must-do's, a list of unacceptable behavior, or a combination of the two. Think of the culture deck as arguably the most important document ever to come out of your organization. While a business plan is likely to sometimes radically change as your company grows and adapts to its customers, a culture deck should be subtly refined but rarely—if ever—overhauled. Why? Because your culture represents the company's values, and these should be non-negotiable.

The most effective culture decks can be read in a few minutes and are written as directly as possible to leave little room for misinterpretation. A culture deck also should be something your organization is proud of and is front and center for all to see (employees, clients, the public, etc.). Transparency with your cultural values acts as the ultimate accountability partner for everyone. It's OK for a business in its infancy to draft a culture deck that is aspirational; however, it must quickly be an accurate reflection of your business.

2. Make Sure Your Values Are for Your Team and Your Team Alone

In a sea of business ideas, it's hard to survive, yet alone differentiate and grow. As most businesses struggle to find an audience and generate attention, it's tempting to think of your culture as a conduit to reach the masses. After all, company culture is a trendy and often discussed topic. Some companies, such as Google and Zappos, have a seemingly never-ending parade of glowing articles written about their very contemporary workplace philosophies. It can be very tempting to build a culture around the latest catchphrases to drum up press and capture the eye of job seekers. When companies do this, it can frequently backfire. Generate a culture deck for political capital alone, and it will quickly vanish, as no one will ever adhere to it. A culture deck is a promise; it's an obligation for the entire company to uphold itself to the highest standards.

3. Develop a Vehicle to Deliver Employee Feedback

How do you know when there's a problem with your culture? You don't—unless you build strong connection points with your team. As an organization scales and employee count increases, it becomes increasingly difficult for a leader to have an accurate pulse on culture and morale. This becomes a particularly arduous task for the leader who has no mechanisms developed to communicate regularly with their team.

Perhaps the best approach to obtain feedback is the diversified one. Start with one-on-one meetings with each team member. Gone should be the days of the annual performance review, the one time a year where management and employees take stock of the last 12 months' worth of work, emotions, and goals—all packaged neatly in a 45-minute conversation. You and each of your leaders should have regular and open communication throughout the year. When done properly, any inklings of cultural malcontent can be identified early before spreading uncontrollably.

In conjunction with one-on-ones, another effective way of staying connected to your team is to set up regular interaction points with them. Town hall meetings, social activities, and team-building events can all prove to be opportunities to not only gel your team but also obtain valuable feedback on the level of happiness from your team.

4. Be a "Level 5" Leader

In *Good to Great*, author Jim Collins introduces the concept of the "Level 5" leader. This most rare and impactful of all leaders looks in the mirror when things go wrong and out the window when things go right. All companies are a product of the hard work and efforts of everyone involved. In fact, the best companies are able to generate more from the sum of its parts than should be possible through basic arithmetic. This can only exist when the leaders at the top share or even deflect the spotlight to their teams. A great company culture is all inclusive to its employees, and when the leader basks in his own glory for too long, the unraveling of the culture begins.

Developing and maintaining a great employee culture should be atop the priority list for any leader worth their salt. One of the most challenging tests of leadership is turning around a struggling culture. Take action on the items above before allowing your culture to veer off course.

PART IV
MANAGING TEAM DYNAMICS— REFLECTIONS

One of the problems you will face as a manager is how you and your organization develop and maintain a culture. If it is a top-down leadership, as in "I'm the boss, so the culture will be what I say it is," you'll be starting by expecting everyone to buy into a culture that may not be the right fit for the organization. This can be a "round peg in a square hole" approach, unless you hire only the square pegs. Then, you may end up with a one-dimensional, assembly-line culture that may not result in much creativity, diversity, or a multifaceted environment.

Conversely, a culture that by some means develops generically may be a wonderful environment in which to work but not built for a profitable, successful business. Therefore, managers are in the position of understanding the global vision as presented by the business owners and leaders and trying to forge a culture that will reach that vision through buy-in from enthusiastic employees who will put in a shared effort and develop a working team dynamic.

It is important that your "living, breathing culture," as discussed in Chapter 22, becomes part of your company but does not take over the role of the business. Culture is important, but it cannot overshadow the business at hand: making money. Therefore, the living, breathing culture may occasionally need a time-out.

As for workplace diversity, discussed by Chidike Samuelson in Chapter 19, it is a widely popular topic. However, a microfocus on diversity can also lead to oversensitivity and an uncomfortable environment for any minority. People want to fit in—not be singled out. For example, introverts, as discussed in Chapter 24, should not be singled out as "an endangered species," who need to be "handled with care." In fact, we have all seen some extroverts speak up, often, boldly, loudly, and clearly at meetings, and elsewhere, who make absolute jerks of themselves. It's easy to think of such a leader if you try.

The Juggling Act

The truth is managers have a lot on their plates. The chapters in this section and throughout this book point to the many aspects of managing people, team dynamics, culture, productivity, and more. The problem that can, and often does, arise, is how much time and focus a manager can put on these without sacrificing other important aspects or responsibilities that come with the job.

Many managers get lost trying to juggle all of the above.

Ultimately, the goal is to carve out enough time to manage each of these many aspects of management in such a way that they adhere to the goals and the future direction of the company. If, and when, a manager is able to fuse all these many responsibilities together so that they no longer have to actively oversee each one, then they have truly mastered the art of management.

Of course, this doesn't mean the culture, team dynamics, or even the bottom line won't change as the company evolves over time with expansion, new employees, technology, and the various needs of the customers. Times will change, and managers will always need to adjust.

RESOURCES

(In Order of Appearance)

Thank you to our talented Entrepreneur contributors whose content is featured in this book. For more information about these contributors, including author bios, visit us at www.entrepreneur.com.

1. Aaron Haynes, "7 Warning Signs You're the Dreaded Micromanager," *Entrepreneur*, March 8, 2017, www.entrepreneur.com/article/289699.

2. Jim Joseph, "Either You Run the Organization or the Organization Will Run You," *Entrepreneur*, November 30, 2016, www.entrepreneur.com/article/285805.

3. Martin Zwilling, "5 Keys to Promoting Accountability in Your Business," *Entrepreneur*, February 24, 2017, www.entrepreneur.com/article/289454.

4. Heather R. Huhman, "Micromanagement Is Murder: So Stop Killing Your Employees," *Entrepreneur*, December 19, 2016, www.entrepreneur.com/article/286333.

5. Karim Abouelnaga, "How to Increase Accountability Without Breathing Down People's Necks," *Entrepreneur*, November 17, 2016, www.entrepreneur.com/article/285376.

6. Larry Alton, "Should You Delegate That? A Comprehensive Guide," *Entrepreneur*, March 8, 2017, www.entrepreneur.com/article/290159.

7. Quentin Vennie, "5 Reasons Why Workplace Anxiety Is Costing Your Business a Fortune," *Entrepreneur*, March 16, 2017, www.entrepreneur.com/article/290530.

8. Tricia Sciortino, "6 Things You Must Do to Effectively Manage Remote Workers,"

Entrepreneur, March 24, 2017, www.entrepreneur.com/article/291026.

9. Dusty Wunderlich, "3 Ways to Decentralize Management and Boost Productivity," *Entrepreneur*, March 15, 2017, www.entrepreneur.com/article/289059.

10. David Adams, "Forget the 'Open Workspace.' Say Hello to the 'Balanced Workspace.'" *Entrepreneur*, July 14, 2016, www.entrepreneur.com/article/278817.

11. Nathan Resnick, "3 Unique Paths to Improving Office Productivity," *Entrepreneur*, March 1, 2017, www.entrepreneur.com/article/289016.

12. Mike Canerelli, "You Can't Afford to Fixate on Results at Any Cost," *Entrepreneur*, February 27, 2017, www.entrepreneur.com/article/289235.

13. Nina Zipkin, "10 Founders Share What Their Worst Boss Taught Them," *Entrepreneur*, January 11, 2017, www.entrepreneur.com/slideshow/287633.

14. Sam Bahreini, "The 5 Touch Points When You Can Boost Retention Through Training," *Entrepreneur*, April 4, 2017, www.entrepreneur.com/article/284955.

Resources

15. Emily Muhoberac, "Tell It Like It Is: Radical Candor Is the Feedback Method Your Startup Needs," *Entrepreneur*, April 3, 2017, www.entrepreneur.com/article/292155.

16. Rehan Ijaz, "5 Reasons Your Employees Shouldn't Fear Making Mistakes," *Entrepreneur*, August 31, 2017, www.entrepreneur.com/article/280656.

17. Rose Leadem, "These Leaders Take Employee Appreciation to the Next Level," *Entrepreneur*, December 28, 2016, www.entrepreneur.com/article/287133.

18. Will Meier, "5 Tips for Giving Better Feedback to Creative People," *Entrepreneur*, March 10, 2017, www.entrepreneur.com/article/290195.

19. Chidike Samuelson, "5 Tips for Dealing Better with Workplace Diversity," *Entrepreneur*, September 14, 2016, www.entrepreneur.com/article/281480.

20. Nicholas Wagner, "Hiring Brilliant Jerks Can Cost You the Culture That Brought Success," *Entrepreneur*, March 22, 2017, www.entrepreneur.com/article/290608.

21. Sherry Gray, "10 Ways Bosses Who Make Nice Bring Out the Best in Their Employees,"

Entrepreneur, November 10, 2016, www.
entrepreneur.com/article/284561.

22. Jayson DeMers, "Why a 'Living and Breathing'
Company Culture Isn't Always a Good Thing,"
Entrepreneur, April 3, 2017, www.entrepreneur.
com/article/292095.

23. Marian Salzman, "5 Generations in the
Workplace (and Why We Need Them All),"
Entrepreneur, February 10, 2017, www.
entrepreneur.com/article/288855.

24. Pratik Dholakiya, "Creating Space for Introverts
to Flex Their Superpower," *Entrepreneur*, April 5,
2017, www.entrepreneur.com/article/292329.

25. Marty Fukuda, "Does Your Company Culture
Match Your Brand?" *Entrepreneur*, March 23,
2017, www.entrepreneur.com/article/290944.

Reader's Notes

Reader's Notes

_____

_____

_____

_____

_____

_____

_____

_____

_____

_____

_____

_____

_____

_____

_____

_____

_____

_____

_____

Reader's Notes

Reader's Notes

_____

_____

_____

_____

_____

_____

_____

_____

_____

_____

_____

_____

_____

_____

_____

_____

_____

_____

_____

_____